THE
AMERICAN
CHARACTER

Forty Lives that Define Our National Spirit

SCOTT RUESTERHOLZ

Post Hill
PRESS

A POST HILL PRESS BOOK
ISBN: 978-1-63758-471-2
ISBN (eBook): 978-1-63758-472-9

The American Character:
Forty Lives that Define Our National Spirit
© 2022 by Scott Ruesterholz
All Rights Reserved

Cover Design by Tiffani Shea
Interior Design by Yoni Limor

Post Hill Press
New York • Nashville
posthillpress.com

Published in the United States of America
1 2 3 4 5 6 7 8 9 10

For all those who dream of creating a better tomorrow, may they take the actions and have the good fortune necessary to realize their dreams and make America and the world better for their endeavors.

Also by Scott Ruesterholz

Robert Wilson and the Invasion from Within

Table of Contents

Introduction

What does it mean to be an American? Of course, it means you are a citizen of the United States of America, either because your parents are American citizens, you were born here, or you've immigrated here from another country. We often hear people proclaim themselves "proud to be an American." But what is it about this country and its history that make us feel proud?

While many nations can trace their history back further than we can, America is actually the oldest continuous democracy on the planet—the only one founded before 1800. Today, the concept of democracy, the idea that the government should be elected by and work for its citizens, is entirely normal. This wasn't always the case. At our founding, it was a controversial and innovative idea. It is a testament to the extraordinary power of the American experiment that democracy has gone from being a radical idea to a normal one.

America has inspired more freedom in more places than ever before; that is a reason to be proud. By encouraging hard work and rewarding success, America is home to unprecedented wealth. Today, Americans are worth over $130 trillion, an unrivaled sum. We have a history of innovation and invention from airplanes to rocket ships and smart phones to search engines.

Of course, these successes were not immediate or uninterrupted. America has faced hardship and challenge. Initially, our call for freedom excluded slaves. It took nearly ninety years after our founding to end the horror of slavery. Over one hundred thousand Americans gave their lives to free the slaves and preserve the union during the Civil War. The price for freedom is often very high. We have suffered recessions and depressions where millions have lost their jobs and many businesses failed. But from the depths of despair, we have always bounced back.

That is the story of America. It is our unyielding pursuit for freedom, liberty, and providing a better life for the next generation, that define us. It is our belief in America that propels us to greater heights and individual acts of bravery.

In 1776, it was the belief in these ideas that led fifty-six men to sign the Declaration of Independence, an act that instantly made them outlaws against the British Empire, the largest in the history of the world.

In 1861, it led over two million men to risk their life to preserve the American Union and end slavery.

In 1941, facing the shock of Japan's sneak attack on Pearl Harbor, the nation rallied to join World War II in the largest and quickest military buildup in history. Within three years, American troops were storming the beaches of Normandy, risking their lives not to conquer Europe but to free it from Nazi tyranny.

In the 1960s, it led countless black Americans to risk their safety to protest segregation and unjust laws and to fight for racial equality.

In 2001, it led hundreds of New York firefighters and police officers to run into the burning World Trade Center on 9/11, risking and sacrificing their own lives to save innocent Americans in the most awful terrorist attack our nation has ever suffered.

This book will help you better understand pivotal moments in American history, our nation's impact on the rest of the world, and why so many feel so proud to be a citizen of this nation. It will do so by exploring a little bit about forty extraordinary Americans, some you know and some you may not. These forty Americans are exemplary figures of the eight defining traits of America: resilience, daring, faith, fairness, sacrifice, drive, industriousness, and innovativeness. Of course, these forty individuals represent a small subset of Americans, and there are many inspiring, influential Americans from Frederick Douglas to Ronald Reagan, who exhibited these traits in their own life, not to mention the countless citizens who make America work and move forward each and every day.

No book could cover the life story of every consequential American; there are far too many. Still, by understanding how each of these forty icons exemplified these
traits (five stories for each) through specific decisions they
made or actions they took in their life, you will better
understand the values America stands for and how this
nation has achieved what it has over the course of its
history. By living these ideals in your life, you can play
your part in ensuring that America's best days lie ahead.

Chapter 1:

Resilience

George Washington

General and President

February 22, 1732 — December 14, 1799

*I*t is only natural that we begin our study of great Americans with George Washington. He became our first president (from 1789–1797) after having successfully overseen victory in the American Revolution. While there were many transformational leaders among our founding fathers, Washington stands at the front of the pack as the father of our nation—the man we consistently turned to from 1775–1789 to lead us from our Declaration of Independence to the ratification of our Constitution.

We might think of Washington today as a man with a golden touch who went from success to success, but that wasn't the case. Before the American Revolution, Washington served as an officer in the British Provincial Militia. In the 1750s, tensions between the world's two leading empires, France and Britain, were steadily rising, culminating in the Seven Years' War. In North America, the conflict was known as the French and Indian War, as French Colonies and their Native American allies fought British Colonies and their own Native American allies. As a result of this conflict, France would turn over territory east of the Mississippi to Britain and Louisiana to Spain.

As this conflict was flaring up, Washington was a lieutenant colonel, making him second in command of three hundred Virginia troops. Ohio Country, which spanned the future state of Ohio as well as portions of Western Pennsylvania, was a key disputed territory between the powers. Washington led one hundred fifty men from Virginia to assess the situation there. At the battle of Jumonville on May 28, 1754, the first battle of the conflict, Washington's forces surprised the fifty Canadian and Native American soldiers, resulting in a quick and total victory.

Following this victory, Washington was promoted to Colonel with the whole of the Virginia regiment as well as one hundred troops from South Carolina joining him at Fort Necessity. All appeared to being going well for Washington. Upon his promotion, Washington began to buttress his position in the Ohio River Country while housing his military supplies at Fort Necessity.

Amid reports of five hundred to six hundred French-allied soldiers amassing in the region, Washington retreated to the Fort and lost the support of his Native American allies, further imperiling his situation. While this was ongoing, Washington's troops worked feverishly to widen the main road through the wilderness to Red Stone Creek to make it easier for British supplies and artillery to move through the region. This proved to be a significant miscalculation, as it made it easier for the French regiment to advance by using this very same road.

By July 3, 1754, the French forces, under the leadership of Louis Coulon, were within sight of Fort Necessity. Over the previous five weeks, Washington's forces had worked through most of their supplies. Washington knew he could not hold off a siege for very long, so he ordered his entire force to charge across the open field to force out Coulon's forces from the woods. While the initial attack worked, many of Washington's forces retreated into the Fort as the French returned fire, leaving him and his men greatly outnumbered. This forced Washington to accept their terms of surrender, abandon the fort, and return with his men to Virginia.

This would be the first of several failures Washington was involved in during the French and Indian War. In 1755, he was a senior aide to British Major General Edward Braddock on his expedition to reclaim Fort Duquesne in the Ohio Country. Washington warned that Braddock's insistence on using standard British tactics of fighting in open fields as "gentlemen" was unwise given how the French forces launched sneak attacks from the woods—a tactic Washington would later emulate when commanding the revolutionary Continental Army. Sure enough, at the Battle of the Monongahela, Braddock and

Washington suffered a stinging defeat with five hundred of their one thousand five hundred troops killed, forcing a retreat.

In 1758, during the Forbes Expedition to reclaim Fort Duquesne, Washington's advice to General John Forbes was ignored. Shortly thereafter, his troops were involved in a friendly-fire incident, fighting other British troops whom they had thought were French. And so following these setbacks, in December of 1758 at the age of twenty-six, Washington retired.

During the French and Indian war, Washington was involved in three major failures. While poor supplies and the refusal of his commanding officer to heed his advice played key roles, many men would lack the self-confidence to involve themselves in military affairs in the future. Fortunately for America, Washington was no such man.

In 1775, as the thirteen colonies began to contemplate declaring their independence from the British Empire, our founding fathers turned to George Washington to lead the Continental Army as its Commander in Chief. The beginning of the war was challenging for Washington, whose troops lost an ill-fated attempt at invading Canada. His forces fell by over half to ten thousand by early 1776 as short-term enlistments expired and soldiers returned home.

As the Declaration of Independence was being signed in Philadelphia, British troops were amassing in New York City in the hope that taking this critical port city could end the rebellion. By this time, Washington had rebuilt his troop strength to twenty thousand, still well short of

British General William Howe's thirty-two thousand men. As Howe's forces approached Washington on Long Island, Washington overruled his generals, believing the British only had eight thousand men based upon intelligence reports. The Continental Army, surprisingly outnumbered, suffered a bruising defeat and the loss of one thousand five hundred men to just four hundred for the British. On August 30, in the dark of night, his forces fled to Manhattan Island. Here, the Colonies suffered another defeat at Fort Washington, eventually sending Washington retreating through New Jersey. Even worse, his army of twenty thousand had been depleted to five thousand four hundred troops in just a few months of fighting.

Washington, who had faced defeat in the French and Indian War just two decades earlier was once again facing defeat after a disastrous start to the American Revolution. However, not only did Washington press on, he had also learned from his past losses. In the French and Indian War, the British often lost because they insisted on traditional open-field fighting tactics rather than launching sneak attacks. Outgunned and outnumbered, Washington's forces deployed a similar strategy. He did this most famously when he crossed the Delaware River on Christmas 1776 and attacked the complacent British forces in Trenton. He won a quick victory, followed by another in Princeton, before settling into his winter headquarters in Morristown, New Jersey.

These victories, coming on the heels of the loss of New York, made clear that the colonies could not quickly be beaten into submission by the British Empire. The army was ragtag, but in Washington, they had a leader who would not be dismayed by defeats. He would press forward relentlessly and adapt strategies as required.

The Continental Army fought on, and by the end of 1777, its numbers under Washington had doubled back to eleven thousand from five thousand four hundred just eighteen months prior. In 1778, France allied with the colonies, giving America further momentum in its war for independence. The war would continue for some time, until the Treaty of Paris was signed in 1783, recognizing the United States of America as a new and free country. Washington resigned his leadership of the Continental Army—a post he held for over eight years—having defeated the largest empire in world history.

Having accomplished his mission, Washington intended to retire into private life. However, after being asked multiple times, Washington agreed to attend the 1787 Constitutional Convention where the US Constitution was drafted with Washington's endorsement. Shortly thereafter, in 1789, George Washington was unanimously elected President of the United States.

As a young man, Washington often faced defeat on the battlefield. It would have been easy to retire to private life on his Mount Vernon estate. He gave up this life to lead the fight for independence, instantly making him an outlaw and traitor in the eyes of the British Empire. In the face of early defeats against a larger and better trained British army, he could have sued for peace and abandoned the effort. Instead, he adapted, learning lessons from his failures, and won small victories that built upon each other. Finally, when his nation needed him once more, he rose to the occasion to oversee the implementation of the US Constitution and serve as America's first president.

Without Washington's resilience, America might not exist today. Washington's fortitude has made him the quintessential American: rising to the occasion, undeterred by past failure, and growing back stronger each and every time.

In 1797, Washington made one last consequential decision, choosing to retire rather than serve a third term as president. Democracies and republics are most fragile in their infancy, and Washington was so popular that he could have been president for life—functionally America's king. Instead, he willingly handed over power to his successor, John Adams. Washington's retirement after two terms became one of the most important precedents in American history with only one president, Franklin Roosevelt, serving a third term. Rather than let power corrupt him, Washington stayed true to his principles and ensured America's young republic would live on. For this, he is not just the quintessential American but perhaps the greatest.

Katharine Hepburn

Film Actress

May 12, 1907 — June 29, 2003

*K*atharine Hepburn was the greatest actress of Hollywood's Golden Era and perhaps in all of cinema's history, boasting a career that spanned over fifty years. Receiving Academy Award nominations in five separate decades, her four wins for Best Actress are the most by any actor or actress, and she won about every award an actress could. In a life filled with such tremendous success, one could falsely assume that it was smooth sailing for her. In reality, her career was nearly derailed just as she was becoming a star. But with resilience, boldness, and hard work, she bounced back to live a life only possible in the movies.

Hepburn was born in 1907 to a wealthy family with her father a successful doctor. Her parents were vocal in sharing their political views, even when unpopular, and her father encouraged his daughters to get educated and fight for their ideals. As a child, she loved the movies and playing sports, becoming an excellent tennis player and golfer; often, she was more comfortable doing "boyish" activities than playing with other girls. This upbringing was critical to the resilience she would display in her career. At Bryn Mawr College, she became involved in the theater, having loved cinema since her childhood, and set out to become a professional actress after graduating.

From 1929–1931, she worked for a variety of small theater productions, finding jobs wherever she could from Baltimore back to Connecticut. In 1932, she won the lead on a Broadway production of *The Warrior's Husband*, which propelled her career forward as RKO Studios signed her to a contract to star in A *Bill of Divorcement*. The film was so successful they signed her to a multi-year contract.

Over the next few years, Hepburn took Hollywood by storm, starring in several smash hits like *Little Women* and winning her first Oscar for *Morning Glory*. Having achieved success in film, she returned to Broadway in 1933, hoping to prove herself just as powerful a star in the theater. This gamble backfired though as her show bombed.

The failure on Broadway would be a turning point in her career and would lead to a series of flops she would suffer over the next few years in film. Films like *Spitfire, The Little Minister, Sylvia Scarlett,* and *Quality Street* were all commercial failures. Her parents had taught her to be outspoken, and so she was in her interactions with the press, making her a lightning rod for controversy. The media hounded her and dubbed her "Katharine of Arrogance."

As the public's view of Hepburn dimmed amid the media's lashing, even her great films faltered. She starred in *Stage Door* and *Bringing Back Baby*, which to this day are viewed as among the finest films ever made. Yet, they failed to connect with audiences, leading movie theater operators to put her on their "box office poison" list. In other words, she had grown so unpopular in the eyes of the public, that her presence in a film undermined its chance for success. Movie theaters did not want Hepburn films anymore.

Seeing the writing on the wall, Hepburn left Hollywood and decided she would have to reboot her career herself. She knew she could be successful; her first films had been an uninterrupted string of successes, after all. So, she signed for a role in a new play, *The Philadelphia Story*, a romantic comedy about a love triangle featuring a feisty socialite replete with laughs and social commentary. She was so confident in the quality of the script that she and her partner at the time, eccentric businessman Howard Hughes, bought the film rights before the play even ran previews.

Beginning with a tour around the country, the stage production was a massive hit with positive reviews. Buoyed by this successful national roadshow, Hepburn returned to Broadway, the place where her career had begun to unravel. There, in the most competitive and ruthless of theatrical markets, the show thrived, running over four hundred performances and sparking a second nationwide tour of the production. By 1939, *The Philadelphia Story* was among the most popular plays in years, and Hollywood was clamoring to put the story on the big screen.

Because Hepburn owned the film rights, no one could make the movie without her approval. She could see the potential for a great career comeback, and she made her appearance as the star a condition of any deal, which MGM Studios, Hollywood's biggest studio at the time, accepted. She chose George Cukor as the director, the man who had directed her first Hollywood film back in 1932. Cary Grant and James Stewart, two of the leading actors of the day, would star alongside her, making the film one of MGM's biggest enterprises of the year.

In 1940, *The Philadelphia Story* opened and became one of the biggest financial successes of the preceding few years while also receiving adulation from critics, including a nomination for Best Picture. Hepburn was back on top. After four years of failures that made her untouchable in Hollywood, she had engineered her own success. To have a comeback like this was in and of itself remarkable, but to do so as a woman, putting her own financial resources into her comeback vehicle, was all the more extraordinary in the 1930s.

Following this success, Hepburn would enjoy newfound success in Hollywood, not just as an actress but as a producer. Her next film, *Woman of the Year*, became another smash hit that netted her at least $125,000 (over

$2 million today) while also introducing her to Spencer Tracy whom she would go on to co-star with in several films and become lifelong romantic partners. Throughout the 1940s, she and Tracy would work together, and beyond the 1940s, she would star in major successes like 1951's *The African Queen*, and she won back-to-back Oscars in 1967 and 1968 for *Guess Who's Coming to Dinner* and *The Lion in Winter*. She would win once more for 1981's *On Golden Pond*.

With forty-eight years between her first win and her last, the longevity of Hepburn's career is without comparison. She maintained relevance in the eyes of the American public for half a century, becoming one of Hollywood's biggest stars before fading into irrelevance and then recovering to become a leading star once again. Her career nearly ended after just five short years, but rather than accept failure, she picked herself up, created her own comeback vehicle in *The Philadelphia Story*, and relaunched a career like no other. In Hepburn's resilience and success, we see America's story.

Steve Jobs

Businessman and Inventor

February 24, 1955 — October 5, 2011

*I*n 2018, Apple became the first private sector company to be valued at over $1 trillion, and then in 2020, it became the first private company to be worth over $2 trillion. Apple is without a doubt one of the most successful companies in American history. Launched in 2007, the iPhone came to redefine what we expect from our cell phones, and it continues to be one of the most dominant smartphones on the marketplace with over two billion devices sold. Much of this success can be attributed to the company's founder, Steve Jobs, who was integral in designing many of the company's products. However, Jobs and the company he founded are only successful because of the resilience they had during times of failure.

Jobs was born in San Francisco in 1955, and he was adopted by Paul and Clara Jobs shortly thereafter. His adopted father was a machinist, and he worked with his son to pass on his skills. At a young age, Jobs showed a proficiency and interest in engineering and electronics. While in high school, he met Steve Wozniak, who was also interested in electronics, and they became best friends. After graduating high school, Jobs attended Reed College but dropped out after a single semester.

Jobs then began working at Atari, a video game maker. During this time, he remained close with Wozniak and worked with him on building a computer, completing the design in March 1976. In April, they founded Apple Computers in Steve Jobs's parents' house, working out of its garage. At the end of the year, they had sold fifty of the computers, generating $25,000 in sales. With an impressive design, Apple was able to get outside investor funding in 1977.

The Apple II would become a major success, and by 1980, Jobs was one of the richest men in America, worth an estimated $250 million. The company continued to thrive into the early 1980s, building a particularly strong market position in the education and consumer sectors. However, Apple struggled to gain much traction against IBM with businesses, and Jobs was focused on beating IBM with Macintosh, a new computer built to give Apple a foothold in the corporate sector. However, the technical limitations of the time made it difficult to produce the closed-architecture platform that Jobs hoped to build for the Macintosh (essentially a closed system not open to other computer manufacturers). Having been so successful at a young age, Jobs was arrogant and uncompromising, becoming a lightning rod of controversy inside of the company. Losing a battle over the future of the company amid the Macintosh's struggles, Steve Jobs resigned in 1985 to launch a new company, NeXT.

In 1990, after five long years, NeXT released its first workstation, but at a cost of $9,999, it was prohibitively expensive. While Jobs could build the technology interface he wanted, it was too costly to be successful. In 1994, the company only made $1.03 million in profits. Meanwhile, without its visionary, Apple was floundering. Throughout the 1990s, the company was steadily losing market share to Bill Gates's Microsoft whose Windows operating system would come to dominate business and consumer computing. In the first quarter of 1996, Apple lost $700 million, in part because it had $1 billion of product that it could not sell. Apple was bleeding cash. Then, at the end of the year, in a shocking turn of events, Apple bought NeXT. In reality, it was just a deal to bring back Steve Jobs.

Apple had been lost without its founder over the previous decade, and NeXT was clearly not going to be a stand-alone success for Jobs either, who was enjoying a better personal financial standing thanks to his majority investment in the animated movie studio Pixar, which had just scored a huge success with *Toy Story*. Apple hoped that by bringing Jobs back, they could rekindle the early magic.

In order to be resilient and bounce back from failures, it is important to learn from them and to be willing and able to change rather than stubbornly repeat mistakes. In 1997, as Jobs took back control of the company, it was in a precarious financial position, its multi-year fight against Microsoft taking a toll. Rather than continuing the costly fight, Jobs shocked the world in August of that year announcing a five-year deal with Microsoft in which they invested $150 million in Apple. Jobs had swallowed his pride and cut a deal with the competition, securing Apple's financial future. Jobs recognized that sometimes compromise is necessary.

By now, the company's technological capabilities had finally caught up to Jobs's vision, and results took off. Its 1998 iMac proved to be a major success, helping the company earn a $300 million profit. Then in 2001, Jobs introduced the iPod and iTunes Store, which quickly became the dominant player in the music industry.

Following this success, Jobs faced a new challenge: his personal health. In October 2003, Jobs was diagnosed with pancreatic cancer, and in 2004, he underwent surgery to have the tumor removed. In 2006, the cancer returned, and while his frail appearance caused rumors, he denied any health issues. Even as his health was deteriorating, Jobs was overseeing the launch of a new product that would turbocharge the company's upward trajectory—the iPhone, which was released in 2007. With a touchscreen and intuitive design, the iPhone would topple the competition to become the dominant smartphone in the market.

In 2009, his health took another turn for the worse, forcing him to take another medical leave of absence, ultimately needing a liver transplant, but he was back to complete work on and launch the iPad in 2010—another revolutionary and highly profitable product.

In the 2000s, by moving beyond computers and into the increasingly mobile world and shunning keyboards in favor of touchscreens, Jobs had put Apple on course to become the leading technology company on the planet. Not only did Apple come back from its failures of the 1990s, it reached new heights. And he did this all while battling major health problems.

Finally, in August 2011, facing declining health, Jobs resigned as Apple's CEO, passing away in October of that same year. The company would continue to thrive in the years after his death, a testament to the enduring strength and popularity of the products he had helped to create. Both Apple and Jobs suffered a failed decade from 1985–1997, with products that went nowhere and had declining relevance to consumers. However, once reunited with the company he helped build, Jobs accepted help from a competitor, which gave him the capacity to explore product lines beyond computers and create extraordinary devices that consumers didn't even know they needed. Jobs is an iconic American entrepreneur because he learned from his failures and bounced back from them, a reminder that our failures only define us if we let them.

Abraham Lincoln

President

February 12, 1809 — April 15, 1865

*A*braham Lincoln was America's sixteenth president and perhaps our greatest. It was his responsibility to save the Union, and after four hard years of civil war from 1861–1865, Lincoln did just that, and in the process freed America's slaves. Unfortunately, his time as president was cut short by a bullet fired by John Wilkes Booth in 1865. We can only wonder how the reconstruction of the Union would have gone if Lincoln's merciful heart and steadfast leadership guided the post-war effort.

By saving America, reuniting the country, and ending slavery, Lincoln stands shoulder to shoulder with the giants of history. Seeing his successful legacy, it can be forgotten that Lincoln, like so many others, faced failure—failures that nearly derailed his career. His resilience allowed him to persevere and eventually ascend to the highest office in the land.

Lincoln was born to a poor family in a log cabin in 1809 and taught himself to read during his childhood in Indiana. Educating himself, he became a lawyer in Illinois. A truly self-made man, Lincoln was elected to the House of Representatives in 1846, at the time a member of the Whig Party.

While Lincoln is remembered for successfully guiding America through her most deadly and traumatic war, another war nearly ended his career in public office. When Lincoln assumed office in 1847, James Polk was the president. On April 25, 1846, about one thousand six hundred Mexican soldiers crossed the Rio Grande into territory disputed by Mexico and the United States. They came across about eighty American soldiers, capturing or killing sixty-six of them.

This attack sparked Polk to ask Congress to declare war on Mexico, alleging they had invaded American territory in the attack. On May 13, Congress approved the war resolution. Lincoln, though, felt that President Polk had misled the American people with his claim Mexico "had shed American blood upon American soil" as the attack may have occurred in disputed territory. His unrelenting focus on the origination of the war resulted in him pushing eight "spot resolutions" during 1847 as a congressman.

Essentially, Lincoln wanted Polk to find and point out the specific spot where the hostilities began to determine if the war had been justified or was started under false pretenses. However, given the conflict had been going on for over a year, it would be extremely difficult to prove conclusively whether American territory had been invaded originally. By late 1947, the US was on the verge of winning the war, increasing its popularity, making Lincoln's focus on its origination all the less popular.

While Polk was celebrated for expanding American territory with Mexico ceding lands that would become California, Nevada, Utah, Arizona, Colorado, and New Mexico, Lincoln had earned the derisive nickname of "Spotty Lincoln." Even though his pursuit of truth was a noble one, it seemed unimportant at the time given the war's outcome. As previously promised, Lincoln chose not to seek re-election, though the mockery he faced for his spot resolutions meant he likely would have lost anyway. So, in 1849, Lincoln left Congress, humbled by defeat and disgusted with politics altogether.

Lincoln then returned to his private law practice, and it would have been easy to enjoy his private life in Illinois. However, he was profoundly troubled by the potential expansion of slavery following the Kansas-Nebraska compromise that would allow northern territories to have slaves if their territory's population preferred it. Rather than be haunted by his humiliating defeat in the Mexican-American War, Lincoln re-entered the public debate as a leader in the new Republican Party.

In 1858, Lincoln ran for Illinois's Senate seat against incumbent Stephen Douglas who had supported measures that expanded slavery. The two would face off in a series of legendary long-form debates during the campaign. Lincoln lost the race, despite Republican legislative candidates winning the popular vote. Lincoln was defeated, but his strong articulation in favor of restricting slavery gave him a national platform.

Once again, rather than wallow in defeat, Lincoln forged ahead. In 1860, Lincoln won the Republican nomination for the presidency. The Democrats nominated Stephen Douglas, the man who defeated Lincoln for Illinois's Senate seat, but the Democrat party fractured over the question of how pro-slavery the platform should be. Lincoln would sweep the Northern states, and despite winning a plurality of just 40 percent, he won an electoral landslide: 180 electoral votes out of 303.

Lincoln persevered through major setbacks. He had gone from being the laughingstock of the nation just thirteen years prior to becoming the President of the United States, during the deepest schism in our nation's history.

Lincoln took office March 4, 1861. Just six weeks later, Southern soldiers fired on Fort Sumter in South Carolina, and America descended into civil war. Lincoln was intimately focused on war planning, building up the Union's military strength, protecting Washington DC from invasion by the Confederacy, and ensuring foreign powers did not assist the Confederates in an effort to weaken America.

At the start of the war, General Winfield Scott, an accomplished military leader, headed the Army. He advocated the "anaconda plan," essentially an effort to block all Southern ports and starve the Confederacy into submission. While the effort would take time, he hoped it would limit bloodshed and give the Union time to build up strength. However, Lincoln and most of the North sought a quicker victory, so he chose a more direct approach.

Lincoln sent troops into Virginia, where his forces were routed at Bull Run, ending any hope of a short and decisive war. Following the disaster of Bull Run, Lincoln appointed George McClellan General-in-Chief, but McClellan was a hesitant leader. Even after the bloody victory at Antietam in 1862 where there were twenty-two thousand casualties, McClellan did not want to chase Confederate troops helmed by General Robert E. Lee, who were retreating through Virginia.

Given his own history, Lincoln was not a man who would bow to setbacks. The first eighteen months of the Civil War were difficult with the Confederacy faring better than anticipated, eliminating hope for a swift reunification. Lincoln tapped into his own resilience to lead the nation and maintain popular support. Throughout 1863, the Union made military gains, most notably the victory at Gettysburg, Pennsylvania.

In 1864, Lincoln promoted General Ulysses S. Grant to lead the war effort, given his battlefield successes against Lee. Finally, after several years, Lincoln had the partner he deserved, and the Union continued to gain momentum in the war. In his re-election campaign, Lincoln faced off against former General McClellan and defeated him easily,

212-21, a strong endorsement of Lincoln's management of the war. Finally, on April 9, 1865, at the Appomattox Court House, General Lee surrendered to General Grant. The Civil War was over. Lincoln and the Union had won; the United States of America had been saved.

Tragically, just five days later, Lincoln was shot at Ford's Theater and passed away shortly thereafter. Without Lincoln, it is far from certain that the Union would have won the Civil War. America could have been permanently divided. Fortunately, he had the resilience to bounce back from personal defeat and re-enter the public arena to help make a more perfect union. That resilience and strength of character would inspire the nation after initial setbacks in the war to persevere and press on. Lincoln's life is proof that we cannot be deterred by missteps. Instead, we can learn from failures and forge ahead to win future victories.

Just weeks before his death, in his second inaugural address, Lincoln urged the nation to reunify "with malice toward none; with charity for all." Lincoln understood the humiliation and indignity the defeated can feel, which is why he knew the nation could only heal if the South faced open arms, not clenched fists. Unfortunately, he could not see that vision through during Reconstruction, though future leaders would learn the wisdom of Lincoln's proposed approach.

For saving the Union, Lincoln is a seminal American leader. His life is a reminder to never give up and let defeat derail your life, for you still can enjoy tremendous success and even change the world.

Ben Hogan
Professional Golfer

August 13, 1912 — July 25, 1997

*P*erhaps more than any other sport, golf is defined by
failure, or more precisely, one's ability to overcome
it. A player is supposed to shoot "par," typically seventy-two strokes over eighteen holes, but few will ever do
so in a lifetime of playing. At the professional level, even
the greatest of players will lose far more tournaments than
they win. If a golfer can win just 10 percent of the tournaments they enter, they will not only be a Hall of Fame
player, they will also go down as one of the greatest players
in history. Unsurprisingly then, one of the greatest stories
of resilience in American sports comes from a golfer. His
name was Ben Hogan.

Hogan was born to a working-class family in Texas
in 1912. When he was nine years old, his father, a

blacksmith, committed suicide, which scarred Hogan for life, potentially contributing to his famed introversion. Needing to make money to help support his family, Hogan's older brother, Royal, dropped out of high school, and Hogan took up a job as a caddie while still attending middle school.

As a caddie, Hogan was introduced to the game of golf, playing during his spare time, and he quickly proved to be a natural. By the age of sixteen, Hogan would pick up any game he could at local public courses to win a few dollars by hustling other players. Confident in his own ability, he dropped out of high school in his senior year and became a professional player just before he turned eighteen in 1930.

Playing golf—or any sport for that matter—for fun is one thing; to play in order to put food on the table is another. In the beginning of his career, Hogan struggled mightily, running out of money a few times. Fortunately, he had a loving wife, Valerie, whom he had met as a teenager, and she stood by him through thick and thin, allowing him to continue. Additionally, in the pre-television era, a career in professional sports was far less lucrative than it is today. A life of luxury was no sure thing; making ends meet was a more pressuring concern for Hogan.

By 1938, after eight years, his career was on an upswing, and he finished in the top fifteen on the money list. Still, he needed to take a job as an assistant professional at a golf club in New York that same year to have a steady income and pay his bills.

Hogan had his breakthrough in 1940, winning his first tournament at the age of twenty-seven. Proving that getting over the hump to win the first time is the hardest, he went on to win his next two events. From 1940–1942, Hogan would go on to win fifteen PGA tour events; his career was on the ascendancy. Thanks to his success during this time, in 1941, Milton Hershey hired Hogan to be the head pro at his golf club—the Hershey Country Club—giving him stability, and he would hold that title for a decade. But then, like many others, Hogan hit pause on his career after 1942, serving in the Army Air Forces during World War II, though he remained stationed stateside in Fort Worth, Texas.

Following the war, Hogan's career continued to thrive; he won five times in 1945. Then in 1946, Hogan had a career season, winning thirteen times, including his first major, a PGA Championship. Hogan was now clearly one of the greatest golfers on the planet. In 1948, Hogan won another ten events, including two majors, a second PGA Championship and the US Open. After a decade of grinding and having to take second jobs during the 1930s, Hogan was now on top of the golfing world. Still, given his very private demeanor, Hogan was not a fan favorite, even as the public respected his great skill.

In 1949, Hogan's year started strong with a win at Bing Crosby's tournament at Pebble Beach in California. But on February second of that year, he and his wife were driving home from the Phoenix Open. While crossing a narrow bridge, a bus going the other direction had moved into his lane to pass another car. With nowhere to veer, they suffered a head-on collision. Instinctively, Hogan threw himself across his wife in the passenger's seat to try and shield her. At the age of thirty-six, Hogan was crippled—his pelvis had broken in two places, and his collar bone, ankle, and a rib were all broken.

Hogan spent the next two months in a hospital, battling complications from his severe injuries, namely a series of deadly blood clots. His doctors told him that they were not sure if he would ever be able to walk again. The golfing world was stunned; it seemed like the world's premiere player would never be able to compete again. But Hogan was determined to prove his doctors wrong. He had worked too hard for his career to end like that. Every day, he walked as far as he could, progressively going a bit further. By November, he was swinging a golf club again. In 1950, he came in second place in his first tournament.

Later in 1950, the US Open was being held at Merion, near the Hershey Country Club. Enjoying the support of a hometown gallery who had a new appreciation for Hogan's grit, he entered the final round two strokes back. Hogan was charging that Sunday, before bogies at fifteen and seventeen endangered his chances. Needing to par eighteen to enter a playoff, he hit his famed one-iron to secure a par and force the playoff, which he would go on to win. Less than two years after being crippled, Hogan was on top of the golfing world once again—an unthinkable triumph.

While his injuries would limit how many events he could play, Hogan continued to dominate when he did play. He won five of the six tournaments he played in 1953, including all three majors he played, earning him a ticker-tape parade down Broadway. To this day, he is the only individual to win the Masters, US Open, and British Open during the same year. All told, Hogan won sixty-four PGA tour events, the fourth most of all time. Eleven of those victories would come after his car accident—an accident that would have been career-ending for most.

After the 1950s, Hogan largely retired from competitive golf, instead becoming an advocate for the game. He would go on to live with his wife Valerie until his passing in 1997 at eighty-four. Facing the longest of odds, Hogan not only bounced back from a devastating set of injuries, but he rose all the way back to the pinnacle of his profession. While among the greatest golfers to ever play the game, his resilience is the truest testament to his strength of character.

Chapter 2:

Daring

Neil Armstrong

Astronaut

August 5, 1930 — August 25, 2012

*B*y 1957, the Cold War between the United States and the Soviet Union was well underway. During World War II, the United States dropped two nuclear bombs on Japan to end the war without having to engage in a costly invasion. The destructive power of these weapons shocked the world and showed America's dominant advantage in military technology. During the 1950s, an arms race began as the US and Soviets built up their nuclear arsenals. The presence of such an arsenal was seen as a way to deter the other nation from launching a preemptive attack. Indeed, the possibility of nuclear conflict kept the US and Soviets from directly engaging in the 1950s' largest proxy conflict, the Korean War, where a young Neil Armstrong would first build a reputation as skilled pilot.

Beyond the arms race, a space race began as the two superpowers sought to assert dominance in space, both for the symbolic victory, as well as the fact that satellites and a space presence could create long-term economic, intelligence, and security opportunities. In 1957, the Soviets shocked the world when they launched *Sputnik*, making it the first artificial satellite in space. The satellite traveled around earth for about three months. Americans could see *Sputnik* fly across the night sky, a reminder that the Soviets had won the first round in the Space Race.

This caused the US to redouble its effort to gain a foothold in space, and shortly after *Sputnik* burned out, America successfully launched its first satellite into space. Later in 1958, President Dwight D. Eisenhower signed into law a bill creating NASA to house all of America's nonmilitary space activity, and we continued to launch satellites.

Then on April 12, 1961, the Soviet Union again shocked the world, sending Yuri Gagarin to space and returning him safely to Earth. He orbited Earth for just under two hours, and the Soviets had won another milestone in the Space Race. This prompted President John F. Kennedy to announce in 1962 that the United States would send a man to the moon and return him to Earth before the end of the decade, an extremely ambitious target that became NASA's primary focus.

The mission would be dangerous; no one knew what would happen to a person if he spent a long time in space or if there might be deadly bacteria or viruses on the moon. Not to mention, a lot can go wrong launching a rocket into space and then hoping to bring it safely back into Earth's atmosphere. For this mission, NASA recruited astronauts, looking for individuals with scientific knowledge and a flying background. Neil Armstrong was one such man.

Armstrong was born in Ohio in 1930 and fell in love with flying as a child, even getting a student pilot certificate before his driver's license. In college at Purdue University, he studied aeronautical engineering and joined the Navy, becoming a naval aviator in 1950. He would fly seventy-eight missions in the Korean War.

After the war and completion of his college studies, Armstrong worked as a test pilot on high-speed military planes, and his unique combination of flying experience and engineering knowledge quickly made him a standout. In 1962, Armstrong applied to be an astronaut for NASA. His application was a week late, but fortunately for him (and for history), a friend slipped it into the pile as though it had arrived on time. Given his stellar credentials, Armstrong was selected along with eight other individuals as part of Project Gemini (later to be renamed Apollo), which sought to put a man on the moon.

Armstrong would spend the next few years training and testing to get into space. In 1966, Armstrong and David Scott took *Gemini 8* into space, becoming the first men to dock to another ship in space, a critical milestone in the effort to reach the moon. However, they then suffered the first major in-space failure as the ship began rolling uncontrollably when a thruster malfunctioned. This forced Armstrong to begin an emergency landing while having burnt up three-quarters of their fuel. Armstrong completed a successful water landing and received an Exceptional Services Medal for his calm control of a dangerous situation.

In 1967, Armstrong was told he would be in first group to land on the moon. He and Buzz Aldrin worked tirelessly over the next two years training for the moon landing and studying the moon's surface to ensure they could safely navigate it. In January 1969, it was publicly announced that Armstrong, Aldrin, and Michael Collins would man *Apollo 11* and go to the moon. Collins would not step foot on the moon, instead orbiting it while Aldrin and Armstrong took the lunar module *Eagle* to the moon's surface.

On July 16, 1969, *Apollo 11* took off without issue from the Kennedy Space Center in Florida to begin an eight-day mission. On July 19, *Apollo* began lunar orbit. Aldrin and Armstrong then boarded *Eagle* on the twentieth to begin the descent to the moon's surface. However, *Eagle*'s computer was going to land the ship into a significant crater, making a safe landing and later departure difficult, so Armstrong took control and successfully navigated the ship past the crater.

They then began to suit up and prepared to exit the craft and touch the moon's surface, a process that took over six hours. Broadcast on television with over six hundred million people watching around the world, Armstrong stepped out of *Eagle* and onto the moon, famously declaring, "That's one small step for man, one giant leap for mankind." They took soil samples and planted an American flag on the moon that remains there to this day. They spent about twenty-two hours on the moon before successfully taking *Eagle* into space, rejoining with Collins, and beginning the safe journey home to Earth.

After returning home, Armstrong retired from NASA and became a professor at the University of Cincinnati. He would pass away in 2012 at the age of eighty-two. Armstrong and all the men and women of NASA broke scientific boundaries, took immense physical risks, and they succeeded in reaching the moon and returning home before the end of the 1960s, scoring the biggest victory of the Space Race. To this day, the United States is the only nation to have put a man on the moon. America was founded by settlers and explorers, and thanks to daring men like Armstrong, we are the leading pioneers of the exploration of space.

Jimmy Doolittle

General

December 14, 1896 — September 27, 1993

On December 7, 1941, Imperial Japan's sneak attack on Pearl Harbor catapulted the United States into World War II. Beyond that, it was a deeply traumatic moment for the nation. It was shocking to see Japan pull off such a crippling attack on an American naval base. Following this strike, Imperial Japan was on the move in the Pacific theater, extending its grip southward. On March 12, 1942, General Douglas MacArthur was forced to evacuate from the Philippines, a significant strategic and emotional blow.

Since Pearl Harbor, America had been put on its back foot while Japan's formidable Naval power seemed unstoppable. There were worries that Japan could invade Australia, or that if its successes in the Pacific continued, it could even launch an invasion of the West Coast. Maintaining morale is critical to any war effort, and President Franklin Delano Roosevelt knew he needed to show a victory—not only to strengthen America's resolve but to shake Japan's. For this project, America turned to Jimmy Doolittle.

Doolittle was born in California in 1896. He was studying at the University of California Berkeley when America entered World War I. He immediately took a leave of absence to serve his country. During the war, he served as a flight instructor, and he also helped patrol the Southern border with Mexico. America had been brought into the war in part due to the intercepted Zimmermann Telegram whereby Germany offered assistance if Mexico invaded the United States, which made protecting the border a national security imperative.

After World War I, he remained in the Air Corps as a reserve officer while also gaining notoriety for his flying ability. For instance, he earned the Distinguished Flying Cross for making the first transnational flight from Florida to California. He was also a strong advocate for the use of instruments in flight to free up the capacity of pilots. He was even the first pilot to complete a flight on instruments alone. By relying on instruments rather than human senses, planes could be flown in all weather, for instance. Instrument flying is the basis of the aviation industry to this day.

In mid-1940, Doolittle returned to active duty as it became clear the US would need to prepare for its potential involvement in World War II. Prior to Pearl Harbor, Doolittle was instrumental in converting automobile plants into plants capable of making the planes the US military would need to fight the war. He served as an emissary between the government and plant management teams in retooling factory floors, coordinating technical requirements in plane design, and retraining workers to ensure product quality and hasten the pace of production. As America prepared for war, leveraging our vast industrial base was critical to building up sufficient military strength.

As the US devised a plan to shock Japan, it was only natural that Doolittle would volunteer to lead the top-secret mission of bombing Tokyo. To this point, Japan's mainland had been untouched by the war. Fighting in the Pacific theater occurred on other islands, in China and the Korea peninsula. The fact that life in Japan felt entirely safe added to that nation's sense of invincibility, a sense Doolittle hoped to eliminate.

To attack Tokyo would be the most daring mission of his career. Doolittle would lead a team of sixteen B-25 bombers and eighty airmen. The journey was too long for planes of that time to make from US soil, so a group of two aircraft carriers brought Doolittle's team out to sea. On the morning of April 18 1942, the Naval task force carrying Doolittle and his team were about seven hundred fifty miles from Japan when they were spotted by a Japanese ship.

This was about two hundred miles further from Japan than Doolittle's team had budgeted. As it was, the journey was a stretch; crews had removed guns from the planes to make them lighter, though this made them more vulnerable to enemy attack. Moreover, none of the pilots had ever actually taken off from an aircraft carrier before—the shortened training period did not allow for it.

The odds of making it to Japan to drop each bomber's load on Tokyo were already low, and they seemed even grimmer now. Doolittle had to decide whether to proceed or scrap the mission. Recognizing the huge psychological stakes, he decided to proceed.

All sixteen planes took off from the carriers without incident, and each made the six-hour journey to Tokyo, bombing their assigned targets. However, given the lengthened journey, there was not sufficient fuel to turn back to the US ships. Instead, they continued westward to China where rebel fighters were engaged in a long-running war with Japan.

Fifteen of the planes crash-landed in China, and one in the Soviet Union. Three soldiers were killed in action, eight were taken prisoner. Sixty-nine survived. At the time, Doolittle was worried that the loss of all sixteen planes—very expensive pieces of equipment—would end his career, but he underestimated the profound psychological impact his attack on Japan would have. The American public was elated to strike back and shock Japan just as they had shocked America in Pearl Harbor. And in Japan, doubts began to fester about the impenetrability of the military defenses, given the apparent ease in which Tokyo was bombed.

In response, due to declining public confidence, the Japanese Navy had to pull forward its planned attack on Midway to June 4, 1942 (less than two months after the Doolittle Raid of Tokyo), to restore its public standing. However, unlike at Pearl Harbor, the American Navy was prepared for this attack. Midway would be among the largest Naval battles of the war, and it was a decisive victory for the United States. Four Japanese carriers were sunk and over three thousand enemy soldiers were killed. By holding Midway, America ensured its ongoing strength in the Pacific and began to turn the tide of the war in the theater. Had Japan not felt hurried into attacking Midway, the conflict and entire trajectory of the war may have been different.

For his role in the raid, President Roosevelt awarded Doolittle the Medal of Honor and promoted him to Brigadier General. During the rest of the war, Doolittle would continue to contribute to the nation's war effort. Most notably, he changed flight strategies in Europe to permit fighter jets to separate from the bombers, allowing them to more easily clear away German resistance and help more bombers successfully reach their target.

Still, the raid on Tokyo was Doolittle's greatest contribution to the nation during World War II. With his daring gamble, he led his men to Tokyo knowing they would lack the fuel to return. By doing so, he restored American morale, and so shook sentiment in Japan, that their Navy would blunder into a costly defeat at Midway.

Samuel Adams

Revolutionary

September 16, 1722 — October 2, 1803

Samuel Adams was born in Boston in 1722. At this time, Massachusetts was, of course, still a colony of the British Empire. Though his parents had twelve children, only three of them would make it to their fourth birthday. His parents raised Sam as a devout Puritan, as most were in Massachusetts at the time. His puritanism would be foundational to his political philosophy throughout his adult life, including the idea of "God-given rights." His parents were active not just in their church but also in local politics with Samuel Adams Senior serving in the Massachusetts House of Representatives.

A strong student, Sam Adams attended Harvard University. Rather than pursue a career in the Puritan Church, Adams continued his studies, and by twenty-one was on the record that it could be lawful for the colonies to resist orders from their British overlords. After college, Adams tried his hand at a variety of business ventures, though none were particularly successful. His family would face financial problems from a British Parliament law dissolving a bank in Massachusetts and making the company's directors personally liable for its currency. Adams Sr. was a director at the bank, which at times led the British government to attempt to seize all of his property. Seeing the British government exert such influence over colonial life further served to move Adams Jr. toward the idea of independence, still a very radical notion at that time.

1748 would be a turning point in Adams's life. That year he founded a newspaper, *The Independent Advertiser*, where he began his political writings, arguing that resistance would be necessary against British encroachment of colonists' rights. His father also passed away that year, giving him new responsibility over his family's finances, and he married his first wife, Elizabeth, all in the same year. Responsibility over a family clarified Adams's thinking about the need to protect the rights he enjoyed from erosion so that his children would enjoy them as well. Politics would consume more and more of his time from this point forward with business interests fading away.

In 1756, Adams was elected Boston's tax collector, though he generally let many avoid paying their taxes. While he personally had to pay some of the shortfall, it greatly boosted his popularity among working class locals who would become the core of his political base. Indeed, issues of taxation would be the spark that would light the flame of the American Revolution.

From 1754–1763, the British had fought the French and Indian War as part of the broader Seven Years' War. While the British won the war, it was very costly, and the British Government was deeply in debt. Parliament was desperate for new revenues into the Royal Treasury, and so, for the first time, they decided to directly tax the colonies. In 1733, the British had imposed a tax on molasses, but it was never enforced. In 1764, the British passed the Sugar Act, which imposed a tax on sugar with severe enforcement mechanisms to ensure revenue would actually be collected this time.

This Act caused a severe downturn in New England's economy as the British West Indies did not face the same tax and were able to undercut New England's exports on price. Adams immediately became a fierce critic of the tax, not only because of its direct economic consequences but also because the colonists had no say, as they had no representation in British Parliament. This second-class citizenship was only acceptable so long as they were not subjected to direct rule. And so, in town meetings, Adams and his ally James Otis Jr. argued against "taxation without representation." Boston would ratify an Adams resolution declaring that Parliament did not have the legal power to impose taxes, laying the groundwork for the legal rationale of independence. To speak so loudly against the British Empire was borderline treasonous; Adams had put himself in England's crosshairs.

Having successfully implemented the Sugar Act, the thirst for tax revenue from the colonies was unquenched, and so British Parliament passed the Stamp Act in 1765, which placed a tax on virtually all printed materials. This tax, which would also serve to make it expensive to speak out against the British Empire by printing pamphlets (the primary means of communication in the 1700s) caused a mass outcry, with more moving to Adams's position that Parliament lacked such sovereignty over the colonies. Associates of Adams would launch violent and disruptive riots around Boston, though he himself had no direct involvement. Resistance against the British was growing. Later that year, Boston sent Adams as their representative to the Massachusetts House of Representatives, solidifying his status as one of the colonies' leading political voices.

In the state legislature, Adams continued to argue that men had natural (or as the Declaration of Independence would later call them, "unalienable") rights which governments could not legally take away. Resistance to the Stamp Act was so powerful that in 1766, the British Parliament repealed it, further boosting Adams's support as well as support for his Popular Party.

In 1767, eager to assert their dominance, the British passed the Townshend Acts, which imposed small tariffs on an assortment of goods. These tariffs were intentionally set to be too small to have a noticeable economic fallout. Rather, the British sought to assert their legal power to tax the colonies and would raise the rates gradually over time. Worse, revenue would support new governors and judges selected by the British. Rather than just "taxation without representation," this was taxation to support oppression.

In response, Adams launched a boycott of British goods, joined by much of Rhode Island and Connecticut. Adams was calling for, and getting, cross-colony coordination. Instead of just viewing themselves as independent entities, colonies were working together, a critical step to the creation of one national identity. By 1768, Boston was completely ignoring the tariffs and trade regulation, and the colonial governor had tried to dissolve the legislature to silence Adams. In October, the British Army began to occupy Boston to enforce the law.

Occupying Boston, the British Army acted with impunity, leading Adams to the conclusion that independence was the only possible course. Tensions boiled over in 1770 when British soldiers killed five civilians during the Boston Massacre. Word spread quickly across the colonies, further boosting anti-British sentiment.

After a several year détente, tensions flared up in 1773 when Parliament passed the Tea Act, which allowed the British East India company to pay no duties under the Townshend Act to increase its colonial business, undercutting local and foreign producers. In response, Adams helped organize the Boston Tea Party whereby colonists snuck aboard British ships and dumped 342 chests of tea into the ocean.

Continued escalation led to the formation of the First Continental Congress, which Adams attended, where he continued to argue for independence, and on July 4, 1776,

Adams signed the Declaration of Independence. For the previous thirty years, Adams had been on the vanguard of the revolutionary movement, pushing the idea of natural rights and representative government that would become foundational American principles. Without men like Adams who dared to challenge the most powerful empire in the history of the world, risking life and property by naming themselves, who knows if America would even exist today.

Olivia de Havilland

Film Actress

July 1, 1916 — July 26, 2020

*A*merica is often described as a nation of immigrants. Very few Americans can trace their heritage to Native Americans, after all. The colonies were largely settled by Europeans, and then, after America's founding, we have welcomed immigrants from all over the world. Since 1850, immigrants have made up 5–15 percent of our population at any given time with first- and second-generation Americans making up a far larger share. Olivia de Havilland is one such American.

De Havilland was born in 1916 in Tokyo to British parents; her mother had been an actress in the theater. In 1919, they were travelling home to England when they stopped in San Francisco because Olivia had fallen ill with tonsillitis. This turned out to be a fortunate turn of events as the family opted to stay in California, letting de Havilland grow up on Hollywood's doorstep.

Having grown up in America, de Havilland became an America citizen in late 1941, just before Japan bombed Pearl Harbor. During the war, no one could doubt her patriotism. She spent the war years raising money for the effort by selling war bonds, serving soldiers at the famed Hollywood Canteen, where Hollywood celebrities gave free meals to troops, and touring the South Pacific on USO tours to raise troop morale. Often, immigrants and their children are among the most patriotic citizens America has, acutely aware of the unique freedoms our nation offers. De Havilland was no exception.

By the time World War II had begun, De Havilland was among the most famous Americans on the planet, for she was one of Hollywood's leading ladies. In the mid-1930s, she was paired with Errol Flynn in smash hits like *Captain Blood* and *The Adventures of Robin Hood*. While these films brought her to prominence, she received widespread acclaim for her role in 1939's *Gone with the Wind*. Adjusting for higher ticket prices today, that film is still the highest grossing of all time, having sold over two hundred million tickets domestically. It was an unrivaled national phenomenon. Still, De Havilland's boldest move would come off screen and revolutionize the American film industry.

Today, actors and actresses have tremendous career flexibility. They choose what films they want to work on, and they turn down roles they don't like. They will work with a variety of directors and for different studios. Simply put, they have the power to pursue the career that they want to. However, that was not always the case; indeed, it is only so because of De Havilland.

In the 1930s and 1940s, the "studio system" dominated Hollywood. The major film studios—Universal, RKO, MGM, and Warner Brothers—signed stars to multiyear contracts. They could only work on that studio's films, and the studio generally picked what role the actors and actresses would take. If there was a better movie at a different studio, the studio they were signed with would "lend" the actor to that studio, often in exchange for another star on one of their own films. However, if no "trade" materialized, the actor could not work on that film.

This system could be burdensome for actors and actresses who wanted to take their career in a different direction and have free artistic expression, but the studios had such control over Hollywood that there really was no alternative, except for a small handful of wealthy independent stars, like Katharine Hepburn, who spent some time independent of the studio system. De Havilland, though, was one of many actresses stuck in and unhappy with the studio system. She had enjoyed great commercial success playing simple roles, typically of attractive, unsophisticated women. She wanted to do roles with complex characters who had real emotional depth so that she could showcase her true acting ability.

In 1943, her seven-year contract with Warner Brothers came to an end, and she was prepared to seek out such roles at another studio. However, as she was preparing to leave, Warner Brothers told her that she had to work for them for another six months because there was a six-month period during the seven years that she hadn't worked. Unlike working as an accountant, where there is always something to do, actors inevitably have some down periods between films, particularly if there is a script they don't like.

Studios had successfully forced actors to accept that a one-year contract did not mean 365 days. If they were not working during part of the contract, the studio acted as though the contract was paused. In this way, studios could lengthen the period in which actors worked for them and coerced them into doing films they otherwise wouldn't because the more roles that one declined, the longer the contract stretched out. Outraged at this, de Havilland decided to fight on the very simple premise that one year means one year.

De Havilland took Warner Brothers to court, seeking to get out of her contract. Sixteen months later, in a landmark ruling in December 1944, the California Appeals Court ruled in her favor, arguing it was common sense that one year is in fact one year and blocked studios' ability to capriciously extend contracts. The ruling sent shockwaves through the industry. Particularly as a woman, de Havilland risked career suicide by fighting the studios who had an incentive to keep the system going. Warner Brothers started a pressure campaign among other studios to not hire her so as to dissuade other actors from exiting their own contracts that had passed their calendar expiration.

Due to this, it took de Havilland two years to work again, but in 1946, Paramount hired her for *To Each His Own*, which gave her the complex role she had longed for, and she would go on to win the Academy Award for Best Actress, a triumphant return to the big screen. After this success, she would become a hot commodity in Hollywood once again.

The De Havilland Law, as it came to be known, came at a critical time, with actors coming home from World War II. Many stars, like Jimmy Stewart (who had once proposed to her), left their existing studio after the war. In combination with an antitrust case brought about by Paramount, the studio system had come crashing down by 1950. De Havilland's legal fight was critical to this and is a notable example of workers fighting for and winning rights.

De Havilland would continue to work for several decades after her legal victory, also enjoying success on Broadway and on television. She risked her career to fight against unfair contract practices. Thanks to her daring action, she enjoyed the career that she wanted to have, and countless American actors and actresses who followed her have enjoyed more legal and artistic freedom, helping to enrich America's culture.

George Marshall

General, Secretary of State, and Secretary of Defense

December 31, 1880 — October 16, 1959

*T*ypically, we associate daring acts with dangerous actions that stretch the imagination. Neil Armstrong's journey to the moon, discussed several pages ago, particularly fits this stereotype of a "daring" action. But, being daring is also about trying to do something that has never been done before, particularly when it flies in the face of everything that is conventional. Doing so, if it goes poorly, can ruin a man's reputation, even if they don't face bodily injury. George Marshall took such an action, and his decision paved the way for the expansion of freedom and American influence over the second half of the twentieth century.

In life, you will often hear the phrase "To the victor goes the spoils." In other words, the winner gets the prize.

We are familiar with this in sports—only the winning NFL team gets to call themselves "Super Bowl Champion." There is no sharing of the honor with the runner-up. The same has been true in war, at least until World War II.

George Marshall was the Army Chief of Staff from 1939 until the end of World War II in 1945. He rose to the rank of General of the Army, a five-star position. It was his job to build up America's military strength as the risk of war rose. Marshall increased the size of the US Army from two hundred thousand men to three million in 1942 and to over eight million in 1945. Marshall coordinated military logistics and plans in Europe and the Pacific, including planning for the invasion of Normandy as America liberated Europe from Nazi rule.

Marshall was a great military leader, instrumental in America's victory in World War II. But his strong planning skills during the war are not why he is included in these pages. History is littered with many great generals, after all. Marshall realized that the peace treaty of World War I played a critical role in the rise of Adolf Hitler and the start of World War II. As was typically the case, the winners of World War I made the losers, namely Germany, pay reparations. In essence, Germany had to pay the cost of the war back to the winners. With its economy already destroyed by the war, these payments led to even further economic crisis and national humiliation. Hitler used this discontent to cement his rise to power.

Marshall did not want to see history repeat itself. Even more pressing, America's ally during the war, the

Soviet Union, was an oppressive power under Joseph Stalin. They retained control over the Eastern European nations they took back from the Nazis, and in their weakened state, West Germany, France, and other free European nations could be vulnerable to Soviet aggression and influence. So, when Harry Truman made Marshall his Secretary of State in 1947, Marshall did the unthinkable.

Marshall laid out a plan whereby the United States, the victor in World War II, would not demand money from the European nations it saved or defeated. Rather, America would hand over money to these nations and help them rebuild. In today's dollars, America gave nearly $200 billion to help Europe rebuild, with most of the funds going to the United Kingdom, France, Italy, and West Germany. By 1952, as the program expired, every participating nation had a bigger economy than they did before the war, something that was unimaginable in 1945.

The Marshall Plan gave Western Europe economic stability, which allowed for the political stability that had been missing after the first World War. With the US even helping West Germany, Marshall made clear that there were no hard feelings over the war. By helping Germany, Marshall essentially harkened back to Lincoln's plea at the end of the Civil War that there be "malice toward none." The past was in the past. While the US provided the reconstruction funds, each nation was responsible for administering their program, a tremendous leap of faith. But giving local control meant that European nations felt empowered rather than ruled over from afar by the United States.

At the same time, Stalin maintained control over Eastern European nations because his occupying forces had installed puppet Communist regimes in the aftermath of World War II. While the US offered aid to these nations, Stalin used his leverage over these governments to block them from accepting funds. This only made starker the divide between America and the Soviet Union as the Cold War began. Stalin chose to harm the economic well-being of Eastern Europeans rather than let them feel close to America. While both were victors in World War II, America and the Soviet Union acted entirely differently. America gave money to help Western Europe get back on its feet while the Soviets ruled harshly over their conquered people.

In the following decades, the economic fate of East and West would diverge. Nowhere was this more apparent than Germany, which remained split for nearly fifty years. West Germany was a free, vibrant nation whereas East Germany was relatively poor and oppressed. In the 1960s, they would resort to building a wall in Berlin to keep their citizens from fleeing to free West Berlin.

Not only did Marshall's plan work in terms of rebuilding Europe's economy and fostering stable democracy, but its true strategic brilliance would take longer to become apparent. By having America rebuild Western Europe, the Marshall Plan fostered more trade between Europe and America, bringing them into our economic sphere of influence. The gratitude for America's support and our shared values made Western Europe an ally in the Cold War. Whereas Europe could have been fertile ground for Soviet expansion, it became a bulwark against Soviet aggression, helping to ensure that America and freedom would prevail in the Cold War. It turned enemies into friends, with West Germany forgiven for the sins committed under Nazi rule, and welcomed as an equal in the community of Western Nations. Similarly, the US, under the stewardship of General Douglas MacArthur, would provide aid to Japan and turn another former foe into a steadfast ally with a thriving economy.

The Marshall Plan was among the most daring feats in diplomatic history. The idea that the winner of the war shouldn't enjoy the spoils of victory but should spend money to help the nation it fought was without precedent. In the halls of diplomacy, Marshall made a bold move, that a show of kindness would be rewarded. Indeed, the Marshall Plan not only helped build up the European economies stronger than ever before, it tilted the balance of power away from the Soviets and formed the foundation of the Western alliance that remains to this day. It is fitting that the man who helped plan D-Day to free Europe also designed the plan to rebuild it.

America's greatest legacy in World War II is that we entered the war not as conquerors but as liberators. As such, the Marshall Plan was the perfect capstone to America's war effort. Marshall had an optimistic, transformative vision of what the world can be and took decisive action to realize it. For that, we all owe him a debt of gratitude.

Chapter 3:

Faith

Alvin York

War Hero

December 13, 1887 — September 2, 1964

*I*n 1916, President Woodrow Wilson won a narrow reelection, 277-254, in the electoral college with a plurality of 49.2 percent of the popular vote. His key campaign slogan was simply: "He Kept Us Out of War." Since 1914, the European Continent had been engulfed in a brutal conflict that we now know as World War I. Begun when Archduke Ferdinand of Austria-Hungary was assassinated, it spiraled into the most inhumane wars, pitting France, Britain, and Russia against Germany, Austria-Hungary, the Ottoman Empire, and Italy. The use of tear gas and machine guns led to brutal trench warfare where thousands of lives were sacrificed just to gain a few yards of territory. Over the course of the war, nearly ten million lives would be lost.

Given the European nature of the conflict, Wilson had averted involvement to that point, but America was coming closer to entanglement. Famously, a German submarine sunk the ocean liner *Lusitania* near Britain in 1915, which was carrying Americans on board. While the Germans had warned Americans not to board the ship, this swung American sentiment further against the Germans. In January 1917, Britain intercepted the Zimmermann Telegram and gave it to Wilson. Germany was urging Mexico to join the war effort against the United States and would finance a war to take back its former Texas territories.

While America had remained neutral to this point, Germany's overture to Mexico was a monumental miscalculation, as it united the public. Within days, Woodrow Wilson called for America to enter World War I by declaring war on Germany. Within months of an election in which he campaigned on keeping America out of war, he was bringing America into war. However, in 1916, America's military had fewer than two hundred thousand soldiers and sailors, among the smallest of the world's major nations. As a consequence, Wilson initiated a draft, eventually growing America's military to over 3.5 million men. Alvin York was one of those draftees.

Alvin York was born in Fentress County, Tennessee in 1887, which was an extremely rural and economically underdeveloped area. His family was poor, and he was born in a two-room log cabin. Alvin spent less than one year in school before he had to quit to help his father on the family farm. In 1911, when his father passed away,

Alvin helped to care for his younger siblings. Aside from working the farm, he worked odd jobs in construction, as a blacksmith, and logging to help ends meet.

Alvin was devoted to his mother and siblings and worked very hard, but he was also an alcoholic with a violent temper and had numerous run-ins with the police for causing disturbances and getting into bar fights. This gave his mother, a devout pacifist Christian, great grief. While York went to church each week to placate his mother, he never was a particularly religious man. However, in late 1914, he had a religious awakening and embraced his family's faith, even giving up drinking.

His church was the Church of Christ in Christian Union, founded during the Civil War, and it opposed all forms of violence. When the US was pulled into World War I, York was twenty-nine years old and registered for the draft. However, his faith led him to seek an exemption on religious grounds, citing the commandment "thou shalt not kill." His first request was denied, but working with his preacher, he decided to appeal the decision.

Pending the appeal, he began training in the 328th Infantry Regiment of the 82nd Division of the army. While training, he stood out as an excellent rifleman. York had been a hunter since a very young age and using a gun had become second nature to him. He was one of the best shots in the company. He and his battalion commander, Major Edward Buxton spent much time debating biblical passages and the merits of York's anti-war position, as Buxton was also a devout Christian. Still, York was troubled about whether he should go to war, so he was given a special ten-day leave to visit home and grapple with his religious conflictions.

While home, he came to the conclusion that the bible permitted him to serve the government in a justified conflict, which World War I was. He returned to the training site in Georgia and resolved to be the best soldier he could be. In 1918, York and his battalion were in France fighting in the Meuse-Argonne Offensive, the thrust of the final Allied offensive of the war, which stretched the length of the entire Western front.

On October 8, York, who had recently been promoted to corporal for his skilled marksmanship and diligent work ethic, was trying to capture a German position near Hill 223 in northeastern France. York was one of seventeen soldiers set to cross into German lines to destroy their machine gun positions. The group snuck around the German lines and captured a large group of German soldiers who appeared to surrender to them.

Suddenly, gunfire rained down upon them, killing six and wounding three, leaving just seven of York's soldiers to try and maintain control over several dozen German prisoners. While his men were under cover, York worked his way around to get a shot on the machine gunners firing upon them. All of his years of shooting as a child in Tennessee paid off. He killed fourteen German soldiers manning the machine gun, sharpshooting one at a time. He then shot and killed six more German soldiers who charged at him in his trench with bayonets.

In one of the most famed acts of heroism of the war, York single-handedly killed twenty German soldiers and took another 132 hostage, leading them and the seven remaining American soldiers back to the American lines. By silencing those German machine guns, he made it significantly easier for the Allied offensive to continue. For his heroism under fire, York was promoted to sergeant and received the Distinguished Service Cross and the Medal of Honor. The French Republic even granted him the Legion of Honor with Marshal Ferdinand Foch of France, the Supreme Commander of the Allied Forces, saying "What you did was the greatest thing accomplished by any soldier of all the armies of Europe."

When York returned home in 1919, he was hailed as a hero. However, he turned down opportunities to cash in on his war record by refusing offers to become a marketing spokesman or endorsing products he didn't use. Nonetheless, in the late 1930s, he used his public stature to argue for the US to fight in World War II against Nazi Germany, and he even tried to reenlist in the Army, though his age made it impossible.

During World War I, York had to reconcile the call for help from his nation with religious teachings he deeply believed in. If not for York's heroism in 1918, the soldiers he saved by taking out the German machine gun likely would have perished, not to mention the lives saved by enabling an easier American advance with the machine guns out of commission. York's ability to find compatibility between America's war effort and his Christian faith saved lives and earned him the gratitude of the nation.

Billy Graham

Evangelist

November 7, 1918 — February 21, 2018

One of the most influential inventions of the twentieth century was mass media, with radios entering most homes by the 1930s and televisions by the 1960s. These inventions revolutionized the way in which politicians, entertainers, and corporate marketers could reach the public. Prior to this, aside from face-to-face interactions, the only way to communicate with large numbers of people was by way of the printed word. In fact, the invention of the printing press by Johannes Gutenberg in 1436 was critical to spreading the word of the Protestant Reformation that led to the formation of Protestant Christian faiths, which broke off from the Catholic Church.

Similarly, the inventions of the radio and television facilitated a new challenge to established religion and an upswing in the evangelical Christian movement, which would go on to play a pivotal role in America's culture throughout the second half of the twentieth century and into the twenty-first century, winning followers from those disaffected from their faith. Many of these evangelical leaders would become associated with the "Religious Right," forming the bedrock of the modern Republican Party. However, Billy Graham stands foremost among America's evangelical leaders as an individual whose moral clarity transcended political divides and earned him admiration from Americans of all faiths and political beliefs.

Graham was born in 1918 on a dairy farm in North Carolina. At the age of sixteen, Graham saw evangelist Mordecai Ham, who converted him to a Baptist and deepened his Christian faith. In 1943, he graduated from Wheaton College with a degree in anthropology, having already been ordained by a Southern Baptist Church in 1939. Also in 1943, Graham married Ruth Bell, to whom he would remain lovingly married to until her passing in 2007.

In 1944, Graham launched a radio program, *Songs in the Night*, which greatly expanded his reach beyond the First Baptist Church in Illinois where he was pastor. By 1948, he had become president of the Northwestern Bible College. It was during this time that he launched the first of his many "crusades." Named for the religious conflicts in the Middle Ages that were used to spread Christianity, Graham launched massive national, and later international, tours to spread the word of God and his view that the Bible contained infallible truths. In 1949, his crusades in Los Angeles became a national phenomenon, and they were so popular that they ran for eight weeks, five more than originally scheduled.

In 1957, Graham ran a New York City crusade where he filled Madison Square Garden every night for sixteen weeks. The most notable of those nights came on July 18, when the Reverend Dr. Martin Luther King, Jr. delivered the convocation, calling for a "brotherhood that transcends race or color." Graham and King had become good friends and King's appearance on stage was a powerful moment, signaling Graham's support for the Civil Rights Movement. Of course, many civil rights leaders, like King, were also men of faith. King and Graham would remain valued friends until King's assassination in 1968.

While having King on stage made Graham's stance on desegregation and civil rights publicly known, he had held those views for some time. After his crusades had been racially segregated in the South in the late 1940s and early 1950s, by 1953, he had desegregated them, ordering ropes separating the sections by race be taken down or he wouldn't go on stage. He also privately urged President Dwight D. Eisenhower to use federal troops to ensure the Little Rock, Arkansas, schools would be desegregated, which Eisenhower later did.

Alongside his touring crusades, Billy Graham launched the non-profit Billy Graham Evangelistic Association in 1950, which managed radio shows, television programs, and provided financial assistance to regions struck by natural disaster. With the tremendous respect he garnered from Americans of all faiths and persuasions, he became known as the "Great Legitimator"—his support gave a cause new gravitas. Just as he signaled support for desegregation in the 1950s by appearing with King, he openly spoke against South African apartheid as early as 1973, building a strong friendship with Nelson Mandela.

Graham would be the first major evangelist to speak behind the Iron Curtain. While the Soviet Union was officially an atheistic nation, religion had persevered there underground, particularly in Eastern European nations like Poland. While there, he preached for peace and an end to the Cold War. In the 1970s through the 1990s, he would preach across Eastern Europe, South America, and Asian nations like China, India, and South Korea where Christianity was not as widespread, making him one of the most recognizable Americans on the planet.

Graham met with every President from Harry Truman through Barack Obama, offering spiritual guidance and advice. His enduring influence in American culture serves as a reminder that faith and morality transcend any particular political view. Accordingly, the American public named Graham on Gallup's "most admired men and women" list a record sixty-one times. In times of division and rancor, he preached kindness and humility. During times of crisis, the nation turned to him for comfort and guidance. He led the prayer service at the National Cathedral on September 14, 2001, as America sought to heal from the terrorist attack three days prior.

Graham would continue to tour at a breakneck pace of crusades through the 1980s, slowing down in the 1990s as he aged and retiring in 2005. By the end of his 417th crusade, Graham had preached in front at least 220 million people. All told, over two billion have listened to Graham over the radio or watched him on television, making him perhaps the most watched and listened to person in history. When Graham passed away in 2018, he was honored as just the fourth private citizen and first religious figure in American history to lie in honor at the United States Capitol.

In 2020, about one hundred million Americans describe themselves as evangelical Christians, making it the largest overarching religious group in America. Billy Graham's crusades and public appearances did much to grow the faith and make it mainstream across American culture by touting a big-tent, tolerant religion, and partnering with the Catholic Church and other leaders like Martin Luther King on social and charitable causes.

These views and the counsel he provided to American leaders of all persuasions gave him deep credibility and unprecedented moral authority. America was founded with the free expression of religion as a founding ideal, and the massive impact Billy Graham has had on our nation's culture is a reminder of how critical that expression has been to our history.

Jackie Robinson

Professional baseball player

January 31, 1919 — October 24, 1972

On April 15, 1947, Jackie Robinson stepped onto the field to play first base for the Brooklyn Dodgers. By doing so, he became the first black man to play Major League Baseball. To this point, baseball had been segregated with black Americans forced to play in the Negro Leagues where salaries were substantially lower and endorsement opportunities far less meaningful. The baseball situation was separate but certainly not equal. That is, until Jackie Robinson came around.

Robinson was born in 1919 in Georgia. When his father left in 1920, his mother moved to California where they struggled to make ends meet. From a young age, Robinson's athletic talent was evident, enabling him to star in basketball, baseball, football, and track in high school, Pasadena Junior College, and then at UCLA.

Like so many Americans, Robinson had to pause his personal life and put his dreams on hold after America was attacked at Pearl Harbor and brought into World War II. In 1944, Robinson's military career was nearly ended when he refused to go to the back of an army bus; he would eventually be acquitted during a court-martial.

When the war was over, Robinson signed for the Kansas City Monarchs, a Negro League Team where he quickly became a star player. At this time, the General Manager of the Brooklyn Dodgers, Branch Rickey, was actively seeking to bring a black player onto his team, both to make it more competitive and to advance the cause of racial equality. However, Rickey knew that there would be a media microscope on the first player, and poor behavior could derail the effort to integrate the leagues. In Robinson, Rickey saw a player good enough for the Dodgers, but Rickey needed to know if Robinson was the right man.

So, when Rickey met with Robinson, he asked how he would respond to the inevitable racist behavior and name-calling that he would face, particularly when travelling on the road and in the South. Robinson asked Rickey, "Are you looking for a Negro who is afraid to fight back?" to which Rickey responded that he was looking for a man "with guts enough not to fight back." Sometimes, the courageous thing to do is to *not* throw a punch or take the bait, but to rise above the hate and behave with dignity and quiet perseverance.

Robinson understood that he needed to set an example, and as unfair as it was, he would face a higher standard for his conduct than other players would. He agreed to always turn the other cheek. And over his career for the Dodgers organization until his retirement in 1956, he would be a star on the field and a model citizen off the field. In fact, his sterling character and approach would lay the groundwork for the successful non-violent approach Dr. Martin Luther King Jr. would master during the Civil Rights movement in the 1950s and 1960s.

While Robinson was a seminal figure in America's push for racial equality, it is critical to understand the deep role his personal faith played in his life, which gave him the strength and inspiration to take on Rickey's challenge to always be the bigger man. Indeed, to turn the other cheek was originally advice from Jesus Christ in the Gospels.

Robinson's mother, Mallie Robinson, was a deeply devout Methodist, who attended church weekly. She was unfailingly kind to all she interacted with. However, as happens to many youths, he became estranged from the church. Particularly given his heavy sports schedule, playing varsity sports at every season, with games on most weekends, he rarely went to church. And like many young men, there were times his temper could get the best of him.

While attending junior college, Robinson confronted white police officers over the unjust detention of his friend. In response, they arrested him, and he was found guilty on a minor offense for being verbally disrespectful to the officer but given a suspended sentence. After this, Reverend Karl Downs, a local preacher at Scott Methodist Church, urged Robinson to control his justified anger and to channel it with forgiveness and understanding. Connecting with Downs, Robinson began going to church again on a regular basis, as he would for the rest of his life. He became very close to Downs, who was a confidante, and he even helped teach Sunday school. Tragically, Downs would die in a motorcycle accident just a few years later.

Like Robinson, Branch Rickey was a devout Methodist, and they bonded and related to each other over religion. Because of their shared faith, Robinson could better understand why Rickey urged him to turn the other cheek. While travelling on the road, Robinson would frequently attend church and seek out the advice of local pastors as he worked to persevere through the challenges, racism, and adversity that he faced. Every night, he would get on his knees and pray to be closer to God. While Robinson did not make a public show of his faith, in private, he remained a devout man until his death in 1972.

Constantly faced with a barrage of hatred, it can be easy to lose one's faith in humanity. For Robinson, his faith became a reservoir of strength. It validated his belief that, like all men and women, he was created in God's image; that no race was better than another. It gave him the moral compass to rise above the hate, turn the other cheek, be the bigger man, and inspire the nation to continue its push toward desegregation and racial fairness. And during the low moments he faced, his faith was something he could lean on to regain hope, whether it was through a quiet night of prayer, a conversation with a local priest, or rereading portions of the Bible, as Robinson was known to do.

After he retired, Robinson continued his work on civil rights, befriending Dr. Martin Luther King Jr. and raising money to help register more black voters while also helping to lift up black businesses, founding Harlem's Freedom National Bank, for instance. Today, there are countless black athletes playing professional sports thanks to the barrier that Jackie Robinson broke. On his tombstone in Brooklyn, Robinson had written: "A life is not important except in the impact it has on other lives." For inspiring the nation with his high moral character and playing a critical role in helping America end segregation, thereby helping millions of minority Americans, we can say that Jackie Robinson led a truly important life. His life is also a testament to how personal faith can help one create societal change.

Elizabeth Ann Seton
Catholic Nun

August 28, 1774 — January 4, 1821

*E*lizabeth Ann Bayley was born in 1774, when America was still part of the British Empire, and her father was a leading surgeon in New York City and Columbia University's first anatomy professor. She was raised in the Episcopal Church, which was America's offshoot of the Anglican Church following the American Revolution. She was well educated, spoke multiple languages and played the piano, and she was deeply religious. In 1794, she married William Seton, a well-to-do merchant, and they lived on Wall Street. She spent much of her time helping the community's poor and serving as a nurse, focusing her efforts particularly on widows and children.

Life was going well until the Seton's trading business suffered, eventually forcing her husband into bankruptcy in 1800 amid French attacks on American ships. Long suffering from tuberculosis, William Seton's financial problems worsened his health as increased stress exacerbated his condition, and he passed away in 1803. At the age of twenty-nine, Seton was a widow with five children.

From 1803–1805, her husband's former trading partners from Italy helped to support her. As she befriended them, she learned about their faith—Catholicism. Outside of Maryland, Catholics were frequently discriminated against in early America, and when she converted to Catholicism in 1805, New York City had just one Catholic church. To support herself, she had started a school for girls, given her own advanced education. However, as word of her conversion spread through New York, most parents pulled their daughters out of the school, undercutting her finances once again. While the First Amendment protected the freedom of religion from infringement by the federal government, many Americans still harbored religious biases. Just to stay in her home and care for her children, Seton rented rooms to girls who were attending a nearby Protestant Academy.

She was preparing to move to Canada where, given French colonization, Catholicism was more widely accepted, when she met Abbot Louis DuBourg who was President of St. Mary's College in Baltimore. The colony of Maryland had been founded by Lord Baltimore as a refuge for English Catholics who faced persecution. Given this history, it remained the center of America's Catholicism at the beginning of the nineteenth century.

DuBourg had fled from France where the Reign of Terror following the French Revolution had caused the persecution and killing of many figures, including religious leaders. In the United States, he hoped to grow the Catholic faith, which was still very small.

At DuBourg's invitation, Seton moved to Maryland in 1809 where she founded St. Joseph's Academy and Free School—it was America's first Catholic girl's school. Seton created all of the textbooks herself, drawing upon the education she enjoyed as a child. Raising money from wealthy converts to support the school, Seton accepted young girls from all families, offering free admission to those who needed it. This effort merged all of Seton's passions: spreading her faith, helping the needy, and educating children, in particular, girls who were not afforded the same opportunity as boys at this time in history.

By creating the first free Catholic school, Seton set in motion religious education in the United States. Religious education systems have been a popular choice for American parents ever since. Today, nearly two million American children are educated in Catholic Schools, a system that can trace its lineage to Seton. About another two million children are educated in religious schools of other faiths.

In addition to starting America's first Catholic School for girls, Seton formed a religious community on July 31, 1809, founding the Sisters of Charity of St. Joseph. Adopting the rules of the existing Sisters of Charity in France, her congregation began with five sisters. Seton's Sisters of Charity was the first congregation of religious sisters in the United States. She trained each sister how to be a teacher, and they all taught at St. Joseph's Academy.

In addition to growing her congregation in Maryland, Seton spread the faith, sending three sisters to open a congregation in New York City to care for orphaned children. Focusing on nursing and helping the poor, Sisters of Charity helped to tend to the wounded during the Civil War and later conflicts while also opening up hospitals and congregations across the country.

By the time Seton died in 1821 at just forty-six, her congregation in Maryland had grown from five to fifty sisters, and they had educated hundreds of girls. Today, there are about forty thousand nuns in the United States, who can trace their history to the first—Elizabeth Ann Seton. Of those forty thousand about four thousand are Sisters of Charity, the congregation she first founded.

Rather than give up her faith because of the biases she faced in New York City, Seton embraced her faith. It flourished and led her to launch the first all-girl Catholic School and Congregation of Sisters. These institutions, as well as other religious institutions that arose in America, have become critical to American life, providing charitable support, health care, and education to millions of Americans. The vibrancy and diversity of America's religious community has been critical to our growth and moral direction as a nation. Much of this is thanks to pioneers like Seton who were not bowed by bigotry but instead sought to overcome it.

In 1975, Pope Paul VI canonized Elizabeth Ann Seton as a Saint. Fittingly, given her role as a trailblazer for Catholic institutions in this country, she was the first person born in the United States to become a saint in the Catholic Church. Inspired by her example, dozens of churches bear her name, and many schools, including Seton Hall University, take their name for her.

While lesser-known today, Seton is among the most consequential religious leaders in American history. The institutions she created in the United States have since grown tremendously, accelerated later by the growth of immigration from predominately Catholic Ireland and Italy in the latter portion of the 1800s. This influx turned Catholicism from a fringe religion to the single most popular denomination by the early 1900s. New York, where Seton faced discrimination and the failure of her business due to her faith, was now a center of Catholicism in the United States. Individuals of all faiths can be inspired by her devotion to charity, tolerance of those with different beliefs, and helping those in need.

Franklin Delano Roosevelt

President

January 30, 1882 — April 12, 1945

*F*ranklin Delano Roosevelt was born in 1882 in Hyde Park, New York, to a wealthy family. His personal faith is a rarely discussed aspect of his life, but he was raised in a devout Episcopalian family, where his father served in the vestry. This means that he was elected by the parishioners to run the finances of the church, ensure its mission was being upheld, and represent it legally in all corporate matters. As a matter of fact, as an adult, like his father, FDR would serve in his parish's vestry.

While often underappreciated, Roosevelt's life and approach to public service is a reminder that faith in America is not simply restricted to belief in God. It is also rooted in faith in the moral courage and good-heartedness of our fellow citizens.

After serving as the Governor of New York from 1929–1932, Roosevelt won the Presidency in one of the largest landslides ever, defeating incumbent Herbert Hoover 472-59 in the electoral college, winning all but six states. At the time, America was battling a severe economic downturn. Spurred in part by the financial crash of 1929, by July 1932, the Dow Jones Industrial Average had lost nearly 90 percent of its value from just three years earlier.

The economic devastation was immense. Factories closed, and global trade came to a halt. Banks failed by the hundreds as depositors scrambled to take out cash. Unemployment passed 25 percent. It would take a decade for the economy to get back on track with many stops and starts along the way. Indeed, the nation would even face natural disasters like the Dust Bowl during the 1930s that would cripple and bankrupt much of the farming community.

During hard times like these, it can be easy for politicians to play into the public's darkest fears, to seek to divide, and to lay blame on others. This occurred across much of Europe during the 1930s. Roosevelt, though, firmly believed in the ability of American citizens to mount a comeback. He set the tone during his first inaugural address in 1933 asserting that "the only thing we have to fear is fear itself." Essentially, he was saying that as long we maintained faith in one another, we could get through the Depression together.

FDR also revolutionized the way a president communicated with the public. Thanks to the invention and mass adoption of the radio during the 1920s, it was easier than ever to communicate directly with the public, and Roosevelt did this often during his "fireside chats." In these thirty radio conversations, FDR conversed with the American public, never speaking down to them, and instead, frankly explaining the serious challenges the nation faced and why he was sure we would overcome them.

During periods of trouble, many leaders might seek to hide information or obscure the true problems out of fear over how the public will react. Instead, FDR trusted the public's ability to understand problems and respond with calm determination rather than fear. His faith in the American people was rewarded with strong backing for his New Deal and a renewed national purpose. While in hindsight some of these projects may not have been the most efficient use of taxpayer funds, FDR's massive public works program brought electricity to the Tennessee Valley and much of rural America and created Social Security to aid the elderly.

In 1936, even as the nation's economy was far from healed, FDR won another landslide, taking all but two states as he won a record 523 electoral votes. Then in 1940, FDR broke the precedent begun by George Washington, successfully winning a third term, this time taking thirty-eight states and 449 electoral votes.

While the worst of the Depression was behind America, a new threat loomed on the horizon. Nazi Germany's invasion of Poland had started World War II in 1939. On December 7, 1941, Imperial Japan launched a surprise attack on America's naval base in Pearl Harbor, bringing America into the global conflict.

During World War II, FDR continued his fireside chats, sharing information with the public and rallying the nation behind a complete and total war effort. As America's men headed off to war, women filled our factories. Factories once used to make automobiles were converted to make planes, tanks, and ammunition. Unemployment fell below 2 percent as the entire nation's industrial base was unleashed in the most powerful and coherent war-making effort ever seen. The US alone accounted for 50 percent of all war production, even though we had just a fraction of the fighting force.

By rallying the public behind a singular mission, FDR unified the nation to a degree we have never seen since. And so, when seeking a fourth term in 1944, he enjoyed another landslide victory, taking 432 electoral votes.

While America was home to many religions, Roosevelt's use of faith as a unifying force is perhaps best seen in his remarks to the nation on D-Day. On June 6, 1944, the Allied Forces landed on the beaches of Normandy in Operation Overlord. D-Day would mark the start of America's effort to free Continental Europe from Nazi oppression. Just before 10:00 p.m. in Washington on June 6, while Allied forces were still trying to take the beaches, FDR addressed the American public. He delivered a speech unlike any other in American history. Rather than offer facts or encouragement, he said a prayer and asked the entire nation to join him in it.

It began, "Almighty God: Our sons, pride of our Nation, this day have set upon a mighty endeavor, a struggle to preserve our Republic, our religion, and our civilization, and to set free a suffering humanity."

Throughout the prayer, he asked for God to lead our forces to victory and accept into his arms those who gave their lives for this noble cause. Finally, FDR concluded by asking, "O Lord, give us Faith. Give us Faith in Thee; Faith in our sons; Faith in each other; Faith in our united crusade."

The D-Day invasion would prove successful, though it would take another year for the war to end. Roosevelt would not live to see America and the forces for freedom prevail. His health steadily in decline, he passed away on April 12, 1945, having served as president for a record twelve years. Vice President Harry S. Truman would ably oversee the end of hostilities.

Roosevelt's faith transcended any particular religion because, more than anything, his Presidency was defined by his faith in the American people. Faith that when confronted with challenges, the public would rise to overcome them rather than crumple in defeatism. And during the defining hours of his presidency—the invasion of Normandy—rather than shy away from his faith, he showcased it, leading the nation in prayer.

By having faith in America, FDR restored Americans' faith in one another, and the knowledge that together we could achieve impossible things. Together, we beat back the Depression and erased the scourge of fascism from the face of the Earth. For his role as the nation's chief motivator and unifier, Roosevelt sits among the pantheon of presidents.

Chapter 4:

Fairness

Harriet Beecher Stowe

Author

June 14, 1811 — July 1, 1896

*I*n the 1800s, political discussion, both in the United States and around the world, was a domain for men. Women were generally expected to be homemakers and nothing more. They were not expected to have informed opinions, and most only had minimal schooling. While it was very much a man's world, Harriet Beecher Stowe had opinions that mattered, and she was intent on making them heard.

Stowe was born to a deeply religious family in Connecticut, the sixth child of eleven. Her mother passed away when she was five, and her father was a famous Calvinist preacher, Lyman Beecher. He published powerful sermons and was engaged in hot-button social debates of the day, from urging the abstention of alcohol to the education of women. As a consequence, Harriet Beecher was able to get the traditional education that most women lacked.

Of course, in the mid-1800s, the greatest social, political, and moral question that faced America was the question of slavery. Her father was involved in a large public discussion known as the Lane Debates on the question of slavery—whether to colonize Africa and move slaves there or to abolish slavery in the United States.

During this time, Beecher met her husband, a deeply religious man named Calvin Stowe. They married in 1836, and she took on his name. He was an ardent abolitionist, and together, they were active in the Underground Railroad, an association of abolitionists that helped to move escaped slaves to safety in free states and Canada, housing numerous slaves in their own home. In 1850, as part of Henry Clay's package of compromise bills attempting to hold the union together, a much harsher Fugitive Slave law was passed, making it significantly harder to smuggle slaves into free states and more severely punishing those who did.

Having housed slaves secretly in her home, Stowe heard countless stories of the horrors of slavery. She realized that many in the North who did not have strong views on slavery may not have been aware of its terrible conditions or were at least intentionally ignorant of it. Similarly, for many in the South, they likely went out of their way not to consider life from a slave's perspective. Stowe was intent on impacting the public discourse by changing the way Americans thought about slavery. To do so, she set about writing a novel, *Uncle Tom's Cabin*. Her husband served as her literary agent, and they began running chapters in installments of an anti-slavery journal in June 1851, continuing for nine months.

When the installments ended, her husband negotiated a deal for it to be published as a stand-alone book in March of 1852. Hoping to sell five thousand copies, it sold three hundred thousand in its first year in the United States and over a million copies in England. Only the Bible sold more copies that year. The novel focuses on a slave family and a slave's effort to escape the cruelty of slavery for the free North. By focusing on the anti-Christian elements of slavery—the heartbreaking separation of families as slaves are bought and sold and the physical cruelty slaves were subjected to—she appealed deeply to the emotions of her readers.

Uncle Tom is a devout and knowledgeable Christian slave who saves the life of a white girl, an act of heroism by a slave that was without precedent in American literature. Another slave, Eliza, is a loving mother who risks her life to flee for the North because she cannot stand to see her son sold to a slave trader. The novelty of the story and the deep humanity, kindness, and love shown by the slaves despite the cruelty they faced had a profound impact on just about anyone who read it.

Harriet Beecher Stowe could not vote or run for public office, but she was horrified by the immorality of slavery, and she found a way to fight for fairness. This powerful novel became the center of the national dialogue, serving to strengthen the anti-slavery sentiments that were already growing in the North. By helping to reframe the debate around slavery and personalize the toll of this institution, she became one of the most prominent advocates for social change. Throughout the 1850s, Stowe used the success of her novel as a platform to give speeches both in the US and abroad on the moral necessity of abolitionism. Her book also spawned popular theatrical reincarnations, which helped to further spread its message even among those who hadn't read it. Some estimate that several million Americans saw *Uncle Tom's Cabin* as a play between 1851 and the Civil War.

Many scholars suggest that the moving anti-slavery portrayals in her novel played a significant role in hardening the North's unwillingness to continue to tolerate slavery. By doing so, some even argue that it contributed to the start of the Civil War, which served to finally expunge the scourge of slavery, a black mark since America's founding, from our land. In 1862, she even met with President Abraham Lincoln, who is rumored to have joked (as was his nature) about her role in starting the war.

After the Civil War, with slavery abolished, Stowe turned her focus to the unfairness in society towards women who were legally second-class citizens. She argued that married women deserved more legal rights, like the right to own property. She continued to use fiction to sway opinion, writing novels like *My Wife and I*, which argued that women should have the right to vote; after all, they are trusted to manage the affairs of the house, which is the most important place for a family. While works like these would become popular and supported the women's suffrage movement helmed by Susan B. Anthony, none would be as impactful or maintain as enduring a legacy as *Uncle Tom's Cabin*.

Stowe passed away in 1896, likely having suffered from Alzheimer's Disease in her final years. In total, she wrote thirty books. While she would die more than twenty years before women received the right to vote, she is among the most impactful women in American history. In a man's world, she found a way to profoundly alter public opinion, not by directly launching a political fight, but by using the written word to appeal to everyone's heart and mind.

Often, art, whether it be music, painting, film, or literature, is seen as a form of social commentary, reflecting upon the ills or excesses of society. Harriet Beecher Stowe used art not just to comment on the most pressing social wrong in America, but to be a vehicle for social change. At a time when support for abolition was growing, she brought the debate further into the culture's mainstream and accelerated its acceptance. Her success is a reminder that there are many ways to fight for fairness and that a single voice can set forth great change.

Susan B. Anthony

Women's Rights Activist

February 15, 1820 — March 13, 1906

Susan B. Anthony was born in Massachusetts in 1820, the second oldest of seven children. Her father, Daniel Anthony, believed all of his children, even his daughters, should be able to be self-sufficient, a radical notion at a time when women were often expected to be nothing more than quiet housewives. He tried to give his children as much education as possible, sending Susan Anthony to a boarding school when she was seventeen to continue her education. However, in 1837, America suffered a depression as a collapse in cotton prices and severe tightening of banks' lending standards caused the American economy to collapse.

The Anthony family, like so many, faced financial ruin. Susan Anthony dropped out of school, and she took a job as a teacher at another boarding school. Later, she would help manage the family farm. The family was deeply committed to fairness and social change, and Frederick Douglass, perhaps the leading voice for the abolition of slavery, often used their farm for meetings. Douglass and Anthony would become lifelong friends.

As a young adult, Anthony became an impassioned supporter of the abolition movement. In 1837, she began collecting signatures for a petition against slavery. She felt so strongly about the movement that she even worked on the Underground Railroad to help slaves escape and enjoy freedom. In 1851, she met Elizabeth Cady Stanton, whom she quickly befriended, and activism became her lifetime passion. The two would become lasting partners in the quest for social change, with Anthony adept at organizing while Stanton focused on writing to persuade the public.

In 1856, Anthony became the leader of New York's American Anti-Slavery Society chapter. She continued to hold meetings up through the outbreak of the Civil War, despite threats of violence and at times, needing police escorts. She supported not just the abolition of slavery but also the end to segregation in favor of equal treatment of black Americans in every regard. This was a position radically ahead of its time with most abolitionists viewing slavery as evil but blacks as inferior to whites.

In 1863, Anthony and Stanton founded the Women's Loyal National League, America's first national women's political organization. It came at a time when women could not even vote. Anthony showcased her talent for organizing, as the group collected four hundred thousand signatures to abolish slavery, furthering the momentum behind the thirteenth amendment.

With the abolition of slavery completed and having used the anti-slavery movement to hone her organizing skills, Anthony next set about her ultimate goal: equality for women and securing the right to vote. She would dedicate the rest of her life to the woman's suffrage movement. In 1866, she and Stanton created the American Equal Rights Association to refocus on women's issues that had been temporarily pushed aside during the Civil War. This group also focused on issues of racial equality with Douglass serving as a leader. At the time, many abolitionists opposed focusing on women's suffrage, preferring not to mix this issue with helping black Americans get more rights, including the right to vote.

By 1869, the debate over whether to focus just on black men's right to vote or also women's right to vote caused the movement to fracture in two. In 1868, Anthony and Stanton founded *The Revolution*, a weekly newsletter that would focus on women's rights, which they used to advocate their views during the split in the women's suffrage movement. Thanks to the skills her father taught her, like accounting, Anthony managed the newsletter finances and operations while Stanton did much of the writing.

At this time, a married women could not sign a contract; only her husband could. Because Anthony was never married, she was able to directly sign legal contracts, securing convention halls or funding agreements for her organizations, which allowed her to more easily manage the movement. Throughout the 1870s, the women's rights movement remained fractured, with Anthony arguing to focus exclusively on the right to vote versus other equality issues. She felt that once the right to vote was secured, it would become substantially easier to win other rights since politicians would have to be attentive to women voters and their interests.

Anthony became the leading figure in the movement, and starting in 1870, she began travelling the country to give speeches to rally the cause. In a typical year, she would make nearly one hundred speeches. In these speeches, she networked with other women who would join her organization, the National Women's Suffrage Association, which she and Stanton had founded in 1869. Throughout her activist career, she maintained a very modest lifestyle, spending just enough to get by, which helped her raise more money for her cause, while others tended to seek personal profit off of their activism.

In 1872, Anthony illegally registered to vote and voted in that year's presidential election. She was arrested and put on trial. It was a brilliant maneuver on her part, as her trial gained national attention, raising her profile and the cause of women's suffrage further. Ultimately, she was ordered to pay a $100 fine, which she never did, and local officials pursued the matter no further.

In 1875, the Supreme Court ruled the constitution did not give women the right to vote, which ended Anthony's strategy of using the courts to achieve her goal of fairness for women. This began the quest for a constitutional amendment—a difficult process as the amendment needed to be passed through Congress, signed by the president, and ratified by three-quarters of states.

Up through the 1880s, Anthony continued to give speeches to build support for women's suffrage. Finally in 1890, the two suffrage organizations that had broken apart in 1869 merged back together into the National American Woman Suffrage Association with Anthony having complete leadership over the organization in 1892. At this point, she was seventy-two years old, but she maintained the schedule of someone half her age, continuing to give one hundred speeches per year. Rather than pay herself a salary, she donated all the proceeds she made from speaking back into the organization.

By the 1890s, Anthony had gone from a radical figure to one who was increasingly viewed as a national icon. In fact, President William McKinley had her to the White House to celebrate her eightieth birthday in 1900. Still, women's suffrage had not yet been secured, even as momentum continued to grow. Many men still opposed giving women the right to vote, and the liquor lobby fought hard against it because they feared women would support the prohibition of alcohol. This worry was pivotal in blocking women's right to vote in 1896 in California, for example.

In 1906, Anthony passed away at eighty-six. While she did not live to see a national right to vote for women, she did win victories in multiple states like Colorado,

Idaho, Utah, and Wyoming. With the nineteenth amendment, women were guaranteed the right to vote. It passed Congress in 1919 and was ratified in 1920. Beginning in fervor after the Civil War, it took fifty-five years to secure women the right to vote. Thanks to Anthony's unrelenting focus, America finally ended one of its largest inequities. America owes a debt of gratitude to Anthony for her unrelenting pursuit of fairness. She made America a more perfect union.

Dr. Martin Luther King, Jr.

Civil Rights Activist

January 15, 1929 — April 4, 1968

*W*hile our nation's history is filled with men and women who fought to make America a more perfect union and live up to its founding ideal that "all men are created equal," Dr. Martin Luther King, Jr. stands foremost among them in the fight for fairness and equality. Nearly one hundred years after the end of slavery, America was still confronting racial inequality, but change was coming.

Across much of the South and parts of the North, many laws, known as "Jim Crow" measures, had been enacted to separate the races and give black Americans less opportunity than their white counterparts. For example, in many communities, black and white Americans went to different schools. While they were supposed to be equal in quality, in reality, black schools generally had far fewer resources and worse educational outcomes. In 1954, in the seminal *Brown v Board of Education* case, the Supreme Court ended this practice. But examples of racial inequality remained across society.

Born in Atlanta, Georgia, in 1929, King was vividly aware of these racial inequities. King's father was pastor of their Baptist church, and significantly grew the church's membership with his compelling sermons. King's father supplemented his son's education at an all-black elementary school by reading Bible verses with him every night. Morehouse College, a historically black college, accepted him at the age of fifteen, and he graduated college at nineteen in 1948. Following in his father's footsteps, he became a reverend in the Baptist church, and he earned a doctorate degree in theology from Boston University.

Throughout his life, King was faced with the daily injustice and humiliation of racial inequality. From purchasing shoes to going to school to drinking from a water fountain, America was simply not as fair a nation as it should have been in the 1930s, 1940s, and 1950s. Constantly faced with these indignities, it is easy to grow angry or dispirited.

King did not succumb to this temptation. Rather, he realized that to make America fairer, he needed to win broad support, beyond just the black community. Peaceful protest that showcased inequities would win more hearts and minds than violence would. King recognized that an open hand rather than a clenched fist was necessary to build the political support for change.

King first became a national figure in 1955. In Montgomery, Alabama, buses were segregated with black Americans forced to sit in the back of the bus or give their seat to a white person. In December of that year, Rosa Parks refused to move to the back of the bus, and for this offense, she was fined fourteen dollars.

In response, King and local leaders organized a boycott of the Montgomery bus system; because black riders accounted for the vast majority of the ridership, the bus system would be financially crippled. Cab drivers even offered below-cost fares to facilitate boycotters' travel to work each day. The boycott to end bus segregation lasted a year. During that time, King's house was firebombed by racist terrorists. In response, King urged calm, quoting Jesus to his supporters, "He who lives by the sword will perish by the sword" and saying "We must love our white brothers, no matter what they do to us. We must make them know that we love them."

That remarkable restraint spoke to how deeply King believed in using peaceful means to achieve racial fairness. Later, King was charged with conspiracy to interfere with business, for which he spent two weeks in jail. King's decision to respond to hate with love and turn himself in, elevated the Montgomery bus boycott into a national story, building more support for King's cause. Finally, in 1956, the Supreme Court would rule the segregation of buses illegal.

Now a national leader, King cofounded the Southern Christian Leadership Conference to serve as the leading force to orchestrate peaceful protest and provide legal support for protesters. King used peaceful protests, from marches to sitting at segregated lunch counters, to raise awareness for racial inequality and generate press coverage.

In 1963, King had perhaps his most influential moment, leading the March on Washington for Jobs and Freedom to build momentum for civil rights legislation. After initially having concerns that the March could be controversial, President John F. Kennedy rallied allies in unions to help transport marchers to Washington and increase turnout. The rally was aimed at broadening the coalition, protesting in favor of civil rights legislation as well as a higher minimum wage.

Over two-hundred-fifty thousand marchers would attend, and on the steps of the Lincoln Memorial, King would deliver his "I Have a Dream" speech. In the speech, he would say, "I have a dream that one day this nation will rise up and live out the true meaning of its creed: 'We hold these truths to be self-evident: that all men are created equal.' I have a dream that one day on the red hills of Georgia the sons of former slaves and the sons of former slave owners will be able to sit down together at the table of brotherhood...I have a dream that my four little children will one day live in a nation where they will not be judged by the color of their skin but by the content of their character."

With a galvanized public and the relentless drive of President Lyndon B. Johnson, Congress would pass the Civil Rights Act in 1964, but King's work was not yet finished. Many Southern states still made it extremely difficult for black citizens to vote, implementing fees, literacy tests, and other barriers. To protest this injustice, King organized a peaceful march on Selma. During the first peaceful March on March 7, 1965 (which King did not attend due to his church duties), protestors were beaten by the police. All caught on film by the national media, the contrasting visuals of peaceful protestors and police brutality outraged the nation and further enhanced public support for the civil rights movement.

Later that month, President Johnson sent in federal officers to ensure the marchers would be protected, and the March 24–25, 1965, protest would have over twenty-five thousand people attend. In August of that year, Johnson signed the Voting Rights Act into law.

King's years of moral clarity, determination, and peaceful protest were instrumental in progressing the civil rights movement and making America a much fairer nation for all of its citizens, regardless of their race. Over the course of his life, Martin Luther King, Jr. was arrested twenty-nine times. His civil disobedience inspired millions of Americans of all races. Tragically, in 1968, King was assassinated in Memphis, Tennessee, while working on the "Poor People's Campaign" to expand economic opportunity for all Americans.

While King's life was unjustly cut short, his legacy continues to inspire Americans. King was among the most important voices for increasing racial fairness in America. His peaceful approach vindicated the idea that massive political change could be achieved through persuasion and coalition-building. Martin Luther King Jr.'s leadership during the civil rights movement was critical to making America a more perfect union for all.

Louis Brandeis

Supreme Court Justice

November 13, 1856 — October 5, 1941

*T*he Supreme Court has seen among its ranks some of the greatest legal minds in the country, both conservative and liberal, activist and originalist, whose decisions have reverberated strongly through America's culture and political life. A Justice on the Supreme Court for twenty-three years, Louis Brandeis stands as one of its giants with a legacy of legal doctrine that extends to the present day.

Brandeis was born in 1856 in Kentucky in a secular Jewish home. His parents had immigrated to the United States from Austria where anti-Semitism was on the rise, and Jewish citizens faced specific, discriminatory taxes. His father visited America and wrote to his family that "America's progress is the triumph of the rights of man," urging them to follow.

As a child, Brandeis was an excellent student, loving politics, reading, and history. His parents fostered in him the importance of getting an education and having cultured debate. In 1875 at just eighteen years old, he went to Harvard law school where he quickly excelled. Brandeis thrived even though his eyesight had largely failed him, forcing him to pay students to read the textbooks aloud to him.

After spending some time in Missouri and clerking for the Chief Justice of the Massachusetts Supreme Court, Brandeis founded a successful law firm with a former classmate, Samuel Warren. By 1889 at just thirty-three years old, he was arguing cases in front of the US Supreme Court. The Chief Justice of the Supreme Court at the time, Melville Fuller, would tell a friend that Brandeis was the most talented lawyer in the Eastern United States.

Given his success and demand for his work, Brandeis could be picky with clients, choosing to not represent clients whom he believed to be in the wrong and seeking to offer wider advice rather than just serving as lawyer on a single case. Having achieved sufficient wealth and success, after 1890, Brandeis began to shift his focus. He had come to feel that often the letter of the law was not serving the interests of the common man against the excesses of big business, so he spent a significant amount of his time lobbying for changes, successfully winning changes to alcohol and transit laws. Following the Gilded Age of the late 1800s, Brandeis, like Teddy

Roosevelt, had grown wary of the power of monopolies and big business, and he helped to stop J.P. Morgan's attempted monopolization of the railroad industry in 1908 as the federal government began to implement and enforce antitrust laws more aggressively.

He also pioneered the concept of "pro bono" legal work. By the early 1900s, he worked on behalf of people and social organizations for free, even when he had to spend hours arguing in court on their behalf. By representing them for free, they had access to a far better lawyer than they could pay for, and he could use their cases to argue for the larger change he thought was needed. Brandeis was among the first to see the possibility of a lawyer serving as a social reformer.

He became a close advisor to President Woodrow Wilson, even arguing for the creation of the Federal Reserve, America's central bank to this day. He successfully lobbied Congress to pass the Federal Reserve Act in 1913. Then in 1916, President Wilson nominated Brandeis to the Supreme Court, sparking a major congressional battle given his public advocacy work. The Senate Judiciary Committee held its first ever public hearing for a Supreme Court nominee for Brandeis, which has since become commonplace. Because of his role as an advocate and reformer, many questioned whether Brandeis would be an impartial judge, fearing he would use his rulings to advance his political views. After a contentious battle, the Senate confirmed him 47-22, making Brandeis the first Jewish American on the Supreme Court.

Once on the Supreme Court, Brandeis quickly found an ideological partner in Justice Oliver Wendell Holmes, particularly on First Amendment issues. During the first world war, there was a revolution in Russia, which overthrew the Tsarist government with a communist one, birthing the Soviet Union. This shocking turn of events put governments across the West on alarm over the potential for communist revolution. Given this backdrop, there was an increasing effort to regulate speech in Western Europe and even in the United States. Considering the First Amendment says that "Congress shall make no law...abridging the freedom of speech...or the right of the people peaceably to assemble," Brandeis and Holmes were troubled by this reactionary trend.

In 1919, a unanimous Supreme Court ruled that the government could restrict speech when there was a "clear and present danger" that a crime could be committed, though Holmes and Brandeis spent the next decade raising that standard higher. Most notably, in *Whitney v. California* in 1927, Brandeis made among the most powerful arguments for the importance of the freedom of speech, arguing that free speech is a necessary precondition for democracy. In the case, Charlotte Whitney was prosecuted for helping to establish the Communist Labor Party of America.

In his opinion, Brandeis argued that a thriving democracy needs citizens to engage publicly and debate the key issues of the day. Only through wide-ranging debate can individuals come to determine their political truths. There can only be a fulsome debate when those with unpopular views feel that they have the right to speak up without facing persecution. Governments that coerce those with unpopular perspectives into silence ultimately stifle genuine public discourse and cause their citizens to disengage from the political process, leading to the corrosion of democracy over time.

On the power of this opinion, California's governor pardoned Whitney of her crime, and the Supreme Court would cite this opinion in future landmark cases, like *Brandenburg v Ohio*, that protected political speech and assembly from government interference.

Aside from free speech matters, Brandeis's largest legacy is on the right to privacy, an idea he first wrote about as a public advocate in 1890. In the Constitution, there is no explicit right to privacy, but during his career, Brandeis argued that it is inferred by the Fourth Amendment, protecting against unreasonable search and seizure, and the Third Amendment, which barred the federal government from quartering soldiers in citizens' homes. For instance, in *Olmstead v. United States*, Brandeis dissented, arguing that a warrant was needed to wiretap someone's phone. Eventually, the Court would reverse course, citing Brandeis's opinion, and require warrants. As technology has evolved to permit new ways to "search" an individual, the premise of Brandeis's right to privacy has been a critical bulwark against excessive government overreach.

In 1939, having made a distinct mark on the legal world's thinking about privacy and speech issues, Brandeis retired from the Court, given his worsening health. From his private sector work, fighting against monopolies, for banking reform, and pioneering pro bono work, to his work as a justice, trying to keep ordinary people free from government coercion, Brandeis worked to create a fairer society and an inclusive democracy that served the needs of ordinary citizens.

Theodore Roosevelt

President

October 17, 1858 — January 6, 1919

*I*n 1899, President William McKinley's Vice President Garret Hobart died, creating an opening on his ticket ahead of the 1900 election. To fill the vacancy, McKinley chose Theodore Roosevelt to be his running mate, one of the most fateful decisions in American political history. After winning a landslide election, McKinley was assassinated in September 1901, making Roosevelt, at forty-two years old, the youngest President in American history.

Prior to the Presidency, Roosevelt had already led an extraordinary life. He was born in 1858 in New York City and suffered severe asthma as a child. Rather than be controlled by it, he became famous for his extremely active and outdoorsy lifestyle, becoming a symbol of "robust masculinity." Beyond this, he was also a tremendous scholar. He attended Harvard College and later became a best-selling historian, writing books such as *The Naval War of 1812*.

In 1884, Roosevelt's wife of four years, Alice, and his mother died within one day of each other, and he wrote in his diary that night, "The light has gone out of my life." So pained by this loss, he virtually never spoke of Alice again. During this time, he was serving in the New York State Assembly, and he focused on anti-corruption issues, uncovering corrupt maneuverings by financier Jay Gould, judges, and local officials.

As his brand of populist conservatism fell by the wayside in the Republican Party and while processing his personal tragedies, Roosevelt pulled back from public life, spending much time in the Dakotas, further cultivating his love of the outdoors and protecting the environment. But he returned to public life serving on the Civil Service Commission, appointed by President Benjamin Harrison in 1893, where he attacked corruption and cronyism in handing out government jobs. His take-no-prisoners approach led many to call him a "bull in a china shop."

Riding his reputation again as a fighter of corruption, he returned to New York City to become President of the Board of Police Commissioners in 1895. A demanding boss, he would even walk officers' beat with them to ensure they were working as hard as they ought to be. He would only hold this job briefly as President McKinley appointed him Assistant Secretary of the Navy in 1897 where he argued strongly for a naval expansion, including new battleships, as he saw war with Spain, particularly over their presence in Cuba, as inevitable. Later as president, he would continue to expand the navy, building out a Great White Fleet that reasserted the Monroe Doctrine of American supremacy in our hemisphere, warding off European interference.

When the Spanish-American War broke out in 1898, Roosevelt resigned from his post and formed the "Rough Riders," a volunteer group to set Cuba free from Spain. He famously led the infantry charge on Kettle Hill, riding horseback at the front, unafraid of incoming fire. He would later receive the Medal of Honor for his heroism during the conflict.

Having become a national icon, he was elected governor of New York before being chosen as McKinley's running mate. Now as president, he had a national platform to pursue his agenda. By 1901, America had become a veritable world power, as seen by our victory in the Spanish-American war, and a manufacturing giant thanks to the second Industrial Revolution. While more powerful and wealthier than ever, there was great inequality resulting from the Industrial Revolution and ensuing Gilded Age where big companies became bigger and more powerful than ever.

As president, Roosevelt called for a "Square Deal" that would ensure fairness for American workers. He called for "three Cs": conservation of natural resources, control of corporations, and consumer protection. Most notably, he became a trust-buster, using the 1890

Sherman Antitrust Act to take action against companies that had become monopolies that could enjoy excessive profit and stifle competition.

Roosevelt launched forty-four antitrust suits, notably breaking up J.P. Morgan's railroad monopoly. Because the limited number of railroads had allowed them to charge excessive rates, Roosevelt also passed the Hepburn Act in 1906 to counter this anti-competitive behavior, thereby making trade and commerce cheaper. Overseas, he was instrumental in building the Panama Canal, making global shipping far less expensive and increasing America's relevance in global trade. He also more closely regulated John Rockefeller's Standard Oil, leading to its eventual breakup in 1911 on the grounds it was a monopoly. By taking these actions, he helped to lower prices for consumers.

Roosevelt also created the Department of Commerce and Labor to protect workers' rights, and he created the Bureau of Corporations (now known as the Federal Trade Commission) to become the government's chief regulator in antitrust matters. Roosevelt was quickly and significantly modernizing America's civil services to keep pace with the greatly changed economic landscape. In addition to expanding the civil services, he held it accountable for corruption as he had done in the 1890s, prosecuting those taking bribes and putting allies into government jobs.

Roosevelt also began setting standards for food and drugs and increased labelling requirements. Famously, he intervened in a coal strike that was crippling the economy to negotiate higher wages and fewer hours on behalf of the workers. He also created the Forest Services and established five national parks, protecting America's environment and giving citizens affordable, beautiful places to vacation. During his two terms in office, Roosevelt radically remade America's governing structure to catch up to fifty years of economic development, giving power back to ordinary workers.

He also used his bully pulpit to argue for greater racial equality saying, "I fought beside colored troops at Santiago [Cuba], and I hold that if a man is good enough to be put up and shot at then he is good enough for me to do what I can to get him a square deal." He also developed a friendship with black intellectual Booker T. Washington; after meeting, he said "The only wise and honorable and Christian thing to do is to treat each black man and each white man strictly on his merits as a man, giving him no more and no less than he shows himself worthy to have." In 1904, Roosevelt won reelection in a landslide, 336-140, though he struggled in the South, as Republicans tended to, with his overtures to Washington causing considerable angst.

His reputation as a fundamentally fair arbiter extended beyond domestic politics into international relations. In 1904 and 1905, Russia and Japan were engaged in a bitter war, whose trench-warfare style would prove to be a precursor for the style of World War I. Turning into a bloody stalemate, which established Japan as a leading global power, Roosevelt arbitrated the Treaty of

Portsmouth, concluding the conflict. For his efforts, he received the Nobel Peace Prize.

Roosevelt stands as one of America's most influential presidents and a leader in the cause of economic fairness, reining in the excesses of monopolies and increasing rights for workers and consumers. As such, his presidency served as the culmination of a fifty-year revolution in America from a regional, agrarian nation to a global industrialized power.

Chapter 5:

Sacrifice

Gerald Ford

President

July 14, 1913 — December 26, 2006

*E*xcluding those who passed away in office, Gerald Ford was the shortest serving President in American history, spending less than three years in the White House. He is also the only person in American history to become President who was never elected President or Vice President. Nonetheless, in his short time, he made an extremely consequential decision that may have ended his political career, very clearly putting the interest of the nation before his own.

Born in Nebraska, Ford spent most of his life in Michigan, eventually becoming a member of the House of Representatives in 1949. During his twenty-five years in the House, Ford rose through the ranks of leadership within the Republican Party, eventually becoming the leader of House Republicans in 1965.

In 1968, Richard Nixon was elected president, and in 1972, he was reelected by a significant margin. However, his vice president, Spiro Agnew, had to resign in 1973 because he had taken bribes as governor of Maryland. Richard Nixon needed a replacement, so he turned to Ford who was very popular in Congress. The Senate easily confirmed Ford by a vote of 92-3, and he became vice president in December 1973. This wide vote margin spoke to the fact that Ford was not a controversial choice and was seen as a man of integrity, even by political opponents.

While this was occurring, the Watergate scandal was exploding. During the 1972 campaign, there had been a break-in of the Democratic National Committee's headquarters at the Watergate Hotel in Washington, DC. On June 17, 1992, individuals working for Nixon's reelection campaign broke in to wiretap the Democrats' phones so that they would know their opponents' strategy. However, the police came and arrested five individuals during the break-in.

While there was never definitive evidence that Richard Nixon knew of these plans ahead of time, he and his administration sought to cover up any ties to the burglary, including blocking an investigation into how the burglary was funded and deleting eighteen minutes of tapes that recorded Nixon's conversations, presumably about Watergate.

As the investigation intensified in 1973, Richard Nixon fired his attorney general and deputy attorney general in October to avoid turning over tapes of his conversations. This action, known as the "Saturday Night Massacre" deepened Americans' unease that Nixon was hiding something and spurred a high-stakes legal battle. On July 24, 1974, the Supreme Court ruled unanimously that Nixon had to hand over the tapes. Respecting the order from another branch of government, Nixon turned over the tapes on July 30. These tapes revealed that six days after the break-in, Nixon personally ordered the cover-up.

This revelation of his abuse of power led to a complete loss of support amongst Congressional Republicans and the American people. Facing a certain impeachment and removal from office, Nixon resigned the Presidency on August 9. He was the first president to resign in American history.

With Nixon's resignation, Gerald Ford became president. On the negative side, he had no electoral mandate, having been confirmed by the Senate into the vice presidency just nine months earlier. On the positive side, he was entirely untainted by Watergate, having not been part of President Nixon's re-election campaign. Ford took over a very divided and dispirited nation. The Watergate Scandal, following the Vietnam War, was a shock to Americans' trust in their government. At the same time, the country faced severe economic pain with high inflation, an oil embargo, a stock market crash, and recession. The Cold War with the Soviet Union was still ongoing. These were among the most tumultuous times in America since the Civil War.

Gerald Ford had a full-time job just battling these problems. As he took office, ending the Watergate crisis, Ford declared, "My fellow Americans, our long national nightmare is over. Our Constitution works; our great Republic is a government of laws and not of men." Within days of taking office, it became clear that the nightmare was not over. Nixon had broken the law, and he was likely to face criminal prosecution. Just as the nation was beginning to heal from Watergate and regain trust in its government, a trial of Nixon could reopen those wounds. Given the likely legal fights, the process could last for years. Rather than Watergate coming to a close in 1974, it could go on until 1980, impairing the government's ability to deal with the other challenges that our nation faced.

So, on September 8, 1974, Gerald Ford pardoned Richard Nixon. This absolved Nixon of any further legal recourse from his actions as president, and it ended the Watergate saga. At the time, it seemed like an act of corruption. Did Nixon resign to make way for Ford because he had been promised a pardon? Given how cynical the American people had become, this was the immediate reaction of many. Ford's approval rating dropped from 71 percent to 50 percent as he immediately went from being viewed as a trustworthy man to a corrupt one.

In reality, prior to Nixon's resignation, Ford had informed the president he would not agree to preemptively grant a pardon. There was no corrupt deal. While one can debate the merits of his decision, Ford acted in what he saw as America's best interest despite knowing it would imperil his own political future. Sure enough, given his weakened standing, Ford faced a spirited primary challenge from California governor (and future president) Ronald Reagan in the 1976 Republican primary. Ford prevailed after a floor fight at the party's convention as neither Ford nor Reagan had won enough delegates during the primary campaign to secure the nomination. This was the last truly contested convention in presidential elections. He then faced Georgia governor Jimmy Carter in the general election.

Carter, a Washington outsider, was untainted by the scandals that had corroded Americans' faith in their government. While Ford ran a spirited campaign, he lost a narrow election, 50.1 percent-48 percent in the popular vote and 297-240 in the Electoral College. In all likelihood, Ford's pardon of Nixon cost him the election.

Ford did what he knew was right to help the nation heal even though he knew it could cost him severely. This was perhaps one of the most courageous acts of sacrifice by an American president. Often, we can only measure a President's true impact with the benefit of time. As time passes and divisions heal, we can better judge if someone did a good job. It is a testament to the wisdom of Ford's action that some of his most vocal critics at the time, like Democratic Senator Ted Kennedy and *Washington Post* reporter Bob Woodward (who helped break the Watergate story), would later laud him for pardoning Nixon.

Ford was president for just 1 percent of America's history, but he played an outsized role. He faced the worst crisis of confidence in the honesty of government in our history. By pardoning his predecessor, he took a personal hit but ensured the wounds of Watergate would heal, allowing the nation to move forward together. For this, he is an American hero. He did what he knew was right even though it cost him his job, and for a time, his reputation. Only with the benefit of hindsight, did we realize how morally courageous he was. His example is one all Americans should strive to follow.

Harriet Tubman

Abolitionist

March 1822 — March 10, 1913

*H*arriet Tubman was born into slavery as Araminta Ross in 1822 in Maryland, though we do not know her birthdate for sure because official records were generally not kept for slaves. During her childhood, many of her siblings were sold to other families, exposing her quickly to one of the harshest cruelties of slavery. While a teenager, a white man accidentally broke her skull when throwing a rock at another slave who was trying to run away. He, of course, faced no punishment.

As a result of this injury, Tubman suffered severe headaches and occasional seizures for the rest of her life. She also began to experience visions after this incident. She attended a Methodist Church every week and believed these visions were a way in which God was communicating to her, like Joan of Arc centuries before.

In 1849, Tubman's owner sought to sell her, but there were no buyers given her past illnesses and injuries. Later that same year, he died, and it was likely his widow would sell her. Fearing this, she and her brothers successfully escaped, but the brothers decided to go back because one had a pregnant wife. Tubman returned with them. Soon thereafter, she escaped again, by herself this time. Over the next few weeks, she travelled through the Maryland woods by night, using the Underground Railroad.

The Underground Railroad was a network of safe houses for slaves fleeing for the North. Abolitionists, often associated with the Quaker faith, gave fugitive slaves a place to hide, food, and clothes, to aid them on their journey. By the time of Tubman's escape, it is likely the Railroad had assisted over fifty thousand slaves, an extraordinary humanitarian effort.

Tubman crossed over into free Pennsylvania, where she was safe, and she settled in Philadelphia where she worked any job she could find to make some money. However, the rest of her family remained stuck in slavery. The recently passed Fugitive Slave Act was also intended to crack down on organizations like the Underground Railroad by implementing harsh punishments for anyone helping escaping slaves. Essentially, the law made it equivalent to abetting theft as slaves were viewed as property, and anyone aiding a runaway could face six months in jail or a $1,000 fine (equal to nearly $50,000 today).

It would have been easy for Tubman who was now a free woman to move on with her life, forget the past, and enjoy the safety afforded her in Philadelphia. However, she could not live with the injustice she had left behind, and she wanted to do everything she could to help more slaves taste freedom. As a consequence, she would spend the next years of her life relentlessly working to help slaves escape, even though it would mean putting herself in constant legal jeopardy, not to mention harm's way.

In December 1850, Tubman covertly returned to Maryland because she learned her niece was about to be sold and separated from the rest of her family. She was able to help her and her children escape and led them from Baltimore to Philadelphia. In 1851, she made two more trips to Maryland, successfully bringing slaves back when she received word that her husband, who was a freedman, had married another woman. When she returned to Maryland to bring him to Philadelphia, he chose to stay with his new wife, breaking her heart.

By this time, it was dangerous for escaped slaves to live even in free states because bounty hunters would hunt and bring them back to their former owners. Indeed, in the 1857 *Dred Scott v Sanford* case, the Supreme Court would rule that black people were not deemed "citizens" under the Constitution and, as such, escaped slaves had no legal protections under the law. (After the Civil War, the Thirteenth and Fourteenth Amendments, which ended slavery and granted citizenship to all "persons born or naturalized in United States," were ratified, negating this terrible court ruling.) Because of this legal environment, Harriet Tubman and others in the Underground

Railroad increasingly took escaped slaves further north and often into Canada to minimize the risk they would ever be recaptured.

From 1850 until 1861, Harriet Tubman made at least thirteen trips back into Maryland. Had she ever been caught, she would have been put back into slavery or, more likely, killed to scare others from escaping. Fortunately, she never was caught, and instead she directly freed seventy slaves and indirectly helped at least another fifty. She likely inspired hundreds more to escape on their own.

Her successes took on a mythical proportion, and she was often referred to as "Moses," who had led the Jews out of slavery in Ancient Egypt to the promised land in the Book of Exodus. Maryland slaveowners were so troubled by her exploits that they offered a reward of over $1 million in today's dollars for her capture. Fortunately for Tubman, they assumed it was a white Northerner who was aiding their slaves' escape, not a former slave who was viewed as so worthless that her former owner could not sell her. During all of the years Tubman worked in the Underground Railroad, she never lost a slave.

When the Civil War broke out, Tubman aided the Union Army, serving as a nurse in South Carolina, where she also assisted fugitive slaves on their way to the North. By 1863, she took on a prominent role. Her years of secret travel for the Underground Railroad had made her adept at covert operations, and she did intelligence work for Colonel James Montgomery, later becoming the first woman to lead an armed charge when she led one hundred fifty black soldiers at the Raid on Combahee Ferry where they freed over seven hundred fifty slaves.

This feat made her a national figure, and she would continue to work for Union forces over the next two years. In addition to her scouting work, she helped convince many liberated slaves to take up arms and fight for the Union Army. Because she was black, Tubman never received a salary for her work for the Union Army and took to baking pies and selling them to soldiers to make money. But that never dissuaded her; she gave four years of her life to the Union cause because she knew that winning the Civil War was critical to ending slavery. In 1899, Congress would pass a bill to give her a pension of twenty dollars per month (about $650 today) to help with the financial hardships she faced. Tubman passed away in 1913.

From 1851 to 1865, during the prime of her life, Harriet Tubman sacrificed her personal safety and any semblance of an ordinary life to help others. She was one of the most prolific members of the Underground Railroad, helping dozens of slaves escape to freedom. Then she became an important member of the Union Army, scouting in Confederate territory, and nursing soldiers back to health. She did all of this knowing that if she was ever caught, she likely would have faced death. Thanks to the sacrifices of people like Tubman, America was able to rid itself of slavery completely in 1865.

Flight 93 Passengers

*W*ould you give your life to save another's? It's a question many people will ask themselves but few will ever have to answer. Most of us like to believe that we would—that we would act heroically in a time of need. However, few are ever actually confronted with the situation. The passengers of United Flight 93 were, and they answered the call with remarkable heroism.

Tuesday, September 11, 2001, started like any other day for most of the passengers of United Flight 93. There were seven members of the flight crew, and thirty-three unsuspecting passengers expecting to leave Newark Airport for a six-hour flight to San Francisco. Among them, though, were four passengers seeking to hijack the plane and cause untold evil.

The flight was scheduled to leave at 8:00 a.m. that morning, but as is so often the case at Newark Liberty International Airport, they were behind schedule and departed at 8:42. It was the only hijacked plane to leave more than fifteen minutes late. This extra delay would be a critical development. At 8:46 a.m., the first plane involved in the terrorist attack crashed into the North Tower of the World Trade Center. At first, the public assumed it was some horrible accident as terrorism was not yet pervasive in the public consciousness.

But at 9:03 a.m., a plane struck the South Tower. It was now unmistakable; these were deliberate attacks on America by planes that had been hijacked. The Pentagon was struck at 9:37 a.m. With it unknown how many planes were going to be hijacked, the government closed the skies at 9:42 a.m., stopping all new flights and ordering those underway to land as soon as possible.

On Flight 93, the hijackers began to take control of the plane at 9:28 a.m., about forty-five minutes into the flight, by taking control of the cockpit. By 9:32 a.m., they had control of the plane and ordered the passengers to sit at the back of the plane. To this point in history, there had been some plane hijacking, primarily to collect ransom. Planes had not been used as weapons before. The hijackers told the passengers that they had a bomb and would blow up the plane if they fought back. This is likely why the hijackers did not face significant passenger resistance on the other flights as most likely assumed it was about ransom.

However, because Flight 93 had been delayed, it was clear that violent terrorism, not ransom, was the motivating force. Over the next few minutes, several passengers like Tom Burnett, Mark Bingham, and Jeremy Glick used the phones on the plane from the back of the seat in front of them to call loved ones and tell them the plane had been hijacked. While doing so, they learned about the other terrorist attacks, which were now national news. Had the plane not been delayed by those forty minutes, allowing them to learn of the other attacks, it would likely have been too late to do anything.

Over the next fifteen minutes, the passengers had to decide what to do. Stay in the back of the plane and hope for a miracle while risking that the plane would be used as a missile to wreak devastation on some other American target. Or, they could try to fight the hijackers and take back control of the plane. Doing so would almost certainly result in their deaths but it could save the lives of people at the hijackers' target.

Based on recordings of these various phone calls, we believe the passengers took a vote, and they voted decisively to fight back. Prior to launching the revolt, several called home to say a final goodbye to their loved ones. Passenger Todd Beamer said "Let's roll," and, using the food cart, the passengers stormed forward up the aisle just before 10 a.m. The hijackers tried to change the pitch of the plane, rolling it left and right, to make it harder for the passengers to move forward, but they moved forward relentlessly. By 10:02 a.m., they had broken into the cockpit, fighting to get control of the plane, which the terrorists had pointed down to the ground.

At 10:03 a.m., flight 93 crashed in Shanksville, Pennsylvania. The passengers of Flight 93 were not cowed by fear but fought back against their evil terrorist hijackers who ran the plane into the ground, killing all on board. In a tremendous act of heroism, these ordinary Americans took back the plane and likely saved several hundreds of lives in the process. They set aside any thoughts they may have had about their own personal safety, any hope of seeing their loved ones again, and sacrificed their lives to protect those of their fellow countrymen.

Unbeknownst to all on board, Vice President Dick Cheney and President George W. Bush had given authorization to shoot down any nonresponsive planes on the assumption that it had been taken by terrorists, which would have added further to the nation's trauma on its most difficult day in decades. If Flight 93 had continued on to the Capitol in Washington DC as planned, the Air Force would likely have tried to intercede, though we cannot know if they would have shot the plane down successfully. Flight 93 was the last of the four hijacked planes to crash; we cannot know if the FAA's decision to ground all flights that day stopped any other hijackings from occurring.

On September 11, 2001, America and the world saw the very worst of humanity. Nineteen Radical Islamic terrorists hijacked four airplanes with the sole goal of killing innocent civilians just going about their daily life in the hope of causing fear and terror among all Americans. They succeeded in striking three buildings and murdering 2,977 people, but they failed to make America cower in submission or give in to fear. Instead, as it always has, the darkest of evils brought out the moral courage of seemingly ordinary citizens—from the New York fire fighters and police officers who entered the Twin Towers to rescue trapped office workers, knowing they may never exit the towers themselves, to the heroic passengers of United Flight 93 who wrested away control of the plane before the terrorists could strike again in Washington DC.

That is the lasting lesson of 9/11. While evil exists and will show itself in the worst ways when least expected, we can overcome together with courage, resolve, and sacrifice. Because of the selfless bravery of Flight 93's passengers, the US Capitol building is still standing. But more importantly, mothers and fathers and brothers and sisters went home to their families on September 11, rather than being killed by that hijacked plane. Hundreds of Americans are alive today and have families of their own because of the actions of the passengers of United 93. May we always strive to prove their sacrifice worthwhile.

James Stewart

Film Actor

May 20, 1908 — July 2, 1997

James Stewart was one of Hollywood's biggest stars in its Golden Era. He was born in Pennsylvania in 1908 to a middle-class family. His father owned a local hardware store, but Stewart's future lied elsewhere. While at Princeton University, he began acting and performed bit parts in small theatres before making it to Broadway. Scouted by MGM, he made his onscreen debut in 1935. By the late 1930s, Jimmy Stewart would become one of America's leading men.

Stewart, a devout Presbyterian, with his soothing voice and disarming smile, played the morally upright everyman like no one else in Hollywood. Battered by the Great Depression, Stewart provided refuge to a weary public—portraying a hero that the public could relate to.

In the late 1930s, Stewart began a career-defining partnership with director Frank Capra. In 1938, he starred in *You Can't Take It with You*, a feel-good romantic comedy, in which he played the son of a banker madly in love with Alice Sycamore, played by Jean Arthur, who came from an eccentric family. The film would win the Academy Award for Best Picture. Stewart followed this up with 1939's *Mr. Smith Goes to Washington*, playing an idealistic man who refused to bow to the corrupt politics plaguing Washington, DC. It was the third most successful film of the year and earned Stewart a nomination for Best Actor.

Then in 1940, Stewart, working alongside Katharine Hepburn in her comeback vehicle, would win the Academy Award for his role in *A Philadelphia Story*, which was the fifth highest-grossing movie of the year. As 1941 began, Jimmy Stewart had enjoyed three of the most successful years Hollywood had ever seen, starring in hugely popular, critically acclaimed smash hits. Like so many Americans, he was likely eager for what was sure to be a very successful few years, but Stewart knew that trouble was brewing on the horizon.

In 1939, Nazi Germany invaded Poland, sparking World War II, and by June 1940, France had fallen. Germany began unrelenting bombing raids on England, having solidified its hold on Continental Europe. Meanwhile in the Pacific, Imperial Japan was on the march, having invaded China in 1937. To this point, President Franklin Delano Roosevelt had kept the United States directly out of the conflict, providing only modest support to England via the Lend-Lease Program in March 1941.

However, as the world was ensnared in a global conflict for the second time in less than twenty-five years, it seemed inevitable that the United States would be forced to get involved at some point. Jimmy Stewart could have ignored the darkness on the horizon; he was in the prime of his career and America's leading man, after all. But fighting for America was in Stewart's blood. His father had served in World War I while both of his grandfathers fought in the Civil War.

In November 1940, Stewart was drafted, but weighting just 138 pounds, he was five pounds too light given his six-foot, three-inch height. Many might have been relieved by this—the military had rejected him and Stewart could go on making movies with his head held high. However, Stewart's conscience would not let him stand by as America was under threat. For the next few months, he worked on gaining weight and in February 1941, he tried again. Now at the minimum weight requirement, he was enlisted in March 1941 to serve in the Air Corps, which would later become the Air Force. James Stewart was the first major Hollywood star to enlist in the army. After 1941, Stewart would not make another film until 1946 due to his service.

With the Japanese bombing Pearl Harbor on December 7, 1941, America was formally brought into the war. At first, the military used Stewart to drive up recruitment, having him appear on radio and do short films. This publicity campaign, buoyed by his name recognition and the surge in patriotism, resulted in one hundred fifty thousand enlistments. But Stewart was not content to serve as a glorified spokesman for the military. He wanted to help America win the war and protect his nation like his father and grandparents had.

Stewart was a talented amateur pilot. Before he enlisted, he already had a private and a commercial pilot license, even competing in a cross-country race in the 1930s. Despite being over the maximum age at thirty-three, Stewart lobbied his way to the frontlines. He was sent to England where he would pilot the B-24, a heavy bomber. From 1943 to 1945, Stewart would fly twenty combat missions over Germany. In his distinguished service during World War II, Stewart would rise to the rank of colonel. He would also receive a Distinguished Flying Cross, which is given for "heroism or extraordinary achievement." Stewart was the most decorated Hollywood star during World War II.

After returning home in 1945, having served his country with distinction, Stewart served in the Air Force Reserves. He would only retire from the Reserves in 1968 when he reached the mandatory retirement age of sixty. In 1959, he was promoted to the rank of brigadier general, the highest rank ever attained by a major Hollywood actor.

Given his low weight, Stewart could have legally avoided military service and enjoyed five years of financial success starring in movies. Once he joined the military, he could have stayed in the safety of the United States, working primarily to boost morale, recruit soldiers, and train pilots. Instead, he demanded to fly combat missions, risking his life. He successfully piloted more than a dozen missions, helping to turn the tide of the war and free Europe from oppression.

Sacrifice comes in many forms, and Stewart, were he alive today, would no doubt argue that his sacrifice paled in comparison to the tens of thousands who lost their lives in the war effort. He never liked to speak about his war record; he was humble like that. But Stewart is emblematic of the millions who, during World War II and other times of crisis, have willingly paused their own life, potentially jeopardizing their career, to serve their nation and the cause of freedom.

Stewart would enjoy commercial and critical success when he returned to Hollywood. From 1946 to 1960, he earned three Academy Award nominations for Best Actor and formed a successful partnership with director Alfred Hitchcock. However, Stewart is best remembered for the first film he made after the war, teaming up with Capra again for *It's a Wonderful Life*. Widely considered among the greatest films of all time, it explores the profound impact a seemingly ordinary life can have on others.

Examining his life and sacrifice during the second World War, we can say that James Stewart led a truly wonderful life, and America is better for it.

James Stockdale

Vice-Admiral

December 23, 1923 — July 5, 2005

A s America's Cold War percolated after World War II, a new theory, known as the "Domino Theory," began to take hold. It was first articulated by President Dwight D. Eisenhower in 1954. Specifically relating to Southeast Asia, Eisenhower worried that if South Vietnam fell to the Communists, other nations would begin to fall too, like dominos. As a consequence, in an effort to maintain the balance of power against the Soviet Union, several US administrations saw it as critical to support South Vietnam, officially formed in 1955, from communist guerrilla fighters sponsored by North Vietnam.

President Eisenhower provided financial assistance and a small US military presence. His successor, President John F. Kennedy, continued to increase America's presence. By the time of his assassination in 1963, sixteen thousand American personnel were stationed in South Vietnam. Kennedy's successor, Lyndon B. Johnson, inherited a precarious situation, which boiled over in an incident when an American destroyer engaged with North Vietnamese crafts in the Gulf of Tonkin. By 1965, the situation in Vietnam had devolved into a ground war that would stretch through the Nixon Administration. There was one man involved in the conflict from its opening salvo to its conclusion; his name was James Stockdale.

Born in 1923 in Illinois, Stockdale enrolled in the Naval Academy in 1943 during the Second World War. A strong student, he graduated in the top quarter of the class, and in 1949, he enrolled to be a Naval Aviator. By 1954, he was a test pilot for the Navy. Thanks to his strong academic background, he also tutored another aviator, John Glenn, in math and science. Glenn would go on to be the first American to orbit the Earth in space.

Stockdale was involved in the Gulf of Tonkin incident when the USS Maddox engaged with North Vietnamese craft. He was one of four F-8 pilots to counterattack the Vietnamese boats, though they scored no hits. He was flying two days later when Maddox thought it had been fired upon again; however, Stockdale saw no Vietnamese boats and believed it to be mistake. Nonetheless, President Johnson ordered an aerial attack on North Vietnamese targets the next day to deter future aggression.

Stockdale remained in Vietnam as tension continued to rise over the next year. He served three tours of duty in

Vietnam and logged over two hundred combat missions. On September 5, 1965, Stockdale was flying a mission into North Vietnam when his plane was hit and severely damaged by enemy fire. He ejected from the plane and parachuted into a village sympathetic to the North. Badly beaten by the locals, he was immediately handed over to the North Vietnamese as a prisoner of war. He was taken to Hoa Lo Prison, which prisoners would dub "the Hanoi Hilton." Stockdale would spend the next seven and a half years of his life in this prisoner of war camp, living under the worst of conditions.

When he was captured, Stockdale was the commander of a Carrier Air Group, which made him the highest-ranking prisoner of war of the conflict. The North Vietnamese did not belong to the Geneva Convention, which aimed to ensure a certain level of civility among warring nations. Signatories of the Convention, like the United States, pledge to give prisoners of war a minimum living standard and promise not to engage in torture. With the Geneva Convention ignored, the North Vietnamese would treat American soldiers with tremendous cruelty.

Because of his high rank, the Vietnamese wanted to break Stockdale in particular. He suffered constant torture and spent four years in solitary confinement with a light bulb on constantly to make sleep impossible. For two of those years, he was restrained in heavy leg irons. They would beat him heavily, breaking his leg twice. During one particularly severe torture session, Stockdale slit his own wrists to make clear he would rather die than give up any information, forcing his captors to stop and save his life.

While the North Vietnamese felt a need to make an example of Stockdale, he felt a need to be an example to other prisoners of war. He created and enforced a code of conduct that all Americans were expected to follow during their stay, limiting the information they shared with their captors and developing secret ways to communicate between cells to ensure that those in solitary confinement could retain their sanity. He became a pillar of strength for all American prisoners, who marveled at his bravery. Once, rather than be brought outside to be paraded around as propaganda, Stockdale beat his own face in with a stool to disfigure it so that the North Vietnamese could not take him outside. These stories became the stuff of legends, giving other prisoners the courage to carry on.

In 1973, as the Americans and Vietnamese reached peace accords, Stockdale and other Americans returned home. For his extraordinary leadership and sacrifice, Stockdale received the Medal of Honor. When he returned home, he could not walk or even stand straight because of the torture he had faced. He retired as a Vice Admiral in 1979.

Ending in a stalemate, over 2.7 million American soldiers would serve in Vietnam in the effort to keep South Vietnam free from communist North Vietnam's aggression. Over fifty-eight thousand American soldiers gave their lives for the cause. It was a brutal war, unlike any the United States had fought before given Vietnam's jungle terrain, which led to guerrilla fighting and constant sneak attacks. Unlike the World Wars, where fighting was focused on well-defined fronts, in Vietnam, violence could start up anywhere. In that regard, it would be a precursor to the wars in Iraq and Afghanistan, which proved similarly protracted.

The Vietnam War was especially controversial during a tumultuous time in American history, amidst the Civil Rights movement and the growing counterculture movement. Many Americans did not believe that fighting in Vietnam was a vital national security interest, and these feelings intensified by 1969 with the implementation of the draft lottery. As such, the Vietnam War resulted in more domestic protests than any other conflict in American history. While the decision-making of our political leaders at the time remains controversial, we can feel admiration for the Americans who served in the war, many of whom sacrificed deeply for their nation. James Stockdale stands high among them.

Intimately involved with the Vietnam War from the very first incident, Stockdale served with honor and dignity, enduring the worst of conditions as a POW, and he was among the last Americans to leave as a result. His life is a reminder of the harshness of war and of the sacrifices American men and women have endured to serve our nation in the Armed Forces. We are a better nation for the lives they led and sacrifices they made, and we are eternally grateful to them.

Chapter 6:

Drive

George Patton

General

November 11, 1885 — December 21, 1945

*W*hen America entered World War II, it was clear the nature of the fight would be very different than in the first World War. World War I was characterized by trench warfare, a slow-moving struggle over inches; so much so that horses were the primary mode of transportation. In fact, only at the very end of the war did tanks enter use. In World War II, Nazi Germany's dominance in tank technology enabled them to master "blitzkrieg" warfare, moving the frontlines miles in a day, in an equally brutal but much faster paced conflict. Given the nature of the conflict, it is no surprise that America turned to George S. Patton to help lead our military response.

Patton was born in 1885 to a family steeped in military tradition. As a child, he was fascinated by military history and knew he wanted to serve in the military. After attending the Virginia Military Institute, like his father and grand-father, Patton secured an appointment to West Point where he thrived, even competing in the 1912 summer Olympics in the pentathlon.

During World War I, Patton served as personal aide to John Pershing who commanded America's forces, but he wanted to command troops in action. He was given control over America's tank school and was the first American soldier to drive a tank. By mid-1918, Patton had been promoted to lieutenant colonel and was in charge of America's 1st Provisional Tank Brigade. He would always personally lead the tanks into battle, inspiring his men with his gusto and courage. In September of that year, Patton was shot in the leg while leading a tank attack on a German machine gun. He continued to command the battle while bleeding for the next hour. His pioneering war record earned him a Distinguished Service Medal and a Purple Heart.

Between World War I and World War II, Patton, now a major, was critical in developing the army's armored division and tank strategy. During this time, he befriended Dwight Eisenhower, even helping him scholastically. After the outbreak of World War II, Patton argued strenuously for expanded investment in armored forces. In 1941, he was promoted to major general, overseeing mass training exercise in the Southeast. Here, he developed his strategy of fast-paced, relentlessly offensive warfare that would earn him the nickname "Blood and Guts."

In 1942, Eisenhower was elevated to Supreme Allied Commander, and he assigned Patton to lead thirty-three thousand men into North Africa. Control of Africa would enable an invasion of Italy and disrupt supplies of oil and commodities to Nazi Germany. Patton landed in Morocco on November 8, 1942 and quickly overran Vichy France's forces. He negotiated an armistice within three days. Further east, American forces were being pummeled by Germany's leading General, Erwin Rommel, so Patton was promoted to lieutenant general and given command over these forces, setting up one of the highest profile battles of the war.

Upon taking command, he immediately instilled discipline and rigor among the demoralized forces, never accepting anything but success. The Tunisia campaign would see the war's greatest tacticians, Rommel and Patton, face off with Patton using the historically German strategies of outflanking opponents. The campaign would last for over six months with Patton prevailing at the Battle of El Guettar, which was the first battle in which the Americans defeated German forces. By successfully pushing the Nazis out of Tunisia, Patton enabled the Allies to begin the invasion of Sicily, known as Operation Husky.

Patton oversaw an army of ninety thousand men on the July 10th landing and personally led his troops into battle. It took less than six weeks to control Sicily. Towards the end of the battle, Patton became embroiled in controversy after he slapped a soldier in a hospital for "battle fatigue." To the uber-driven and aggressive Patton, this was dereliction of duty. His friend Eisenhower suppressed the incident, and even Patton's political opponents knew that his aggressive instincts were valuable in the war, even if they were socially unpalatable.

Still, Patton would not command forces in combat for nearly all of the next year. However, his reputation continued to grow, particularly within Germany, for his ability to defeat Rommel. As a consequence, as Eisenhower and George Marshall began preparations for the invasion of France in Operation Overlord, they used Patton as a decoy. Adolf Hitler assumed that Patton would oversee any invasion forces, and Eisenhower knew there were German spies throughout England. As Patton was training his Third Army in England in early 1944, they let word leak out that he would invade Pas-de-Calais, even hiring British set designers to build a fake army in rural England. As a consequence, when the Allied Forces invaded Normandy, Hitler resisted sending additional troops, assuming it was a diversion from the "real" invasion led by Patton that never came. This helped buy the Allies crucial time to gain a foothold in France.

In July 1944, with the invasion of Normandy successful, Patton returned to combat, leading his Third Army east. With the largest scout and intelligence team, Patton zoomed across France, leading the Allies' breakout from Normandy and trapping several hundred thousand German troops within two months. The only thing that would stop Patton would be a lack of supplies. Moving sixty miles in under two weeks, his forces had outrun supply lines and run out of fuel, forcing Patton to hold for much of September, which allowed the Germans to rebuild their strength.

In late 1944, the Germans launched the Battle of the Bulge, their last major offensive, which sought to break through the Allies' lines. However, Patton had begun to move his divisions in preparation for a major offensive of his own. This planning allowed for a swift counterattack that quickly relieved the besieged American troops at Bastogne and ended the Nazis hopes of breaking back through France. In 1945, Patton's Third Army advanced through Germany, facing less and less resistance as the war came to an end.

Between August 1, 1944, and the end of the war in May 1945, Patton's Third Army of about three hundred thousand men killed, captured, or wounded over 1.8 million German soldiers, freed over twelve thousand towns, and captured eighty-one thousand square miles (equal to half of California). No other American battle commander has ever been as successful as Patton.

On December 8, 1945, just a few months after the war, Patton was involved in a car accident in Germany, and he died thirteen days later. He was buried in Luxembourg alongside casualties of his Third Army. A man of gusto and controversy who loved battle, George Patton's relentless drive to taste victory was instrumental in freeing a continent from fascism.

Henry Clay

Senator, Secretary of State, and Speaker of the House

April 12, 1777 — June 29, 1852

*A*s America moved forward into the 1800s, it became time for a new generation of leaders to guide the nation. By 1820, America's founding fathers had largely passed away or entered retirement, and most Americans had been born after the American Revolution. The nation was continuing its great expansion westward. By 1820, the number of states had nearly doubled to twenty-four. American politics was dominated by the admission of new states and territories, managing the continued tension between slave states and free states, and guiding the economy as it became steadily more industrial and less agricultural.

In this era from the war of 1812 nearly to the Civil War, three men, Daniel Webster, John C. Calhoun, and

Henry Clay, would form the "Great Triumvirate," striking deals in Congress that would help the Union carry on. Clay was born a year after America's founding, 1777, in Virginia. His father died when he was just four years old. His mother remarried, and he would be one of sixteen children. A lawyer, Clay moved to Kentucky where he built a plantation and owned upwards of fifty slaves. In 1810, the Kentucky legislature selected Clay to serve in the United States Senate (at this time senators were chosen by state legislatures and not voted in directly by citizens).

Clay entered politics with a strong vision for what America ought to be and an unrelenting drive to see his vision come to life in what he called "the American System," which prioritized nationalist economic policies and greater federal integration. Primarily, he sought high tariffs to protect American industry from foreign competition. Second, the US economy was still dominated by intra-state activity, and he wanted to greatly expand interstate commerce to develop one cohesive national economy.

Today, you can use dollars in all fifty states; it is the only legal currency in America. But in the early 1800s, each bank could have their own currency backed by gold. Clay was a strong proponent of a national bank with one national currency to foster commerce between states. This policy would be critical to integrating state economies and is an essential aspect of the American economy to this day. Last, he supported aggressive federal investment in infrastructure to make it easier to transport goods and trade between states. At his core, Clay wanted to make America feel like one nation rather than a collection of associated states.

Realizing that the US Senate was a slow-moving and debate-driven body, he made the unusual decision later in 1810 to seek election to the US House of Representatives, generally seen as a weaker position given only a two-year term versus six years in the Senate and the greater number of representatives than senators. However, his gamble proved wise. When he entered the House in 1811, Clay was voted in as Speaker of the House by his fellow Representatives, instantly making him one of the most powerful men in America.

At that time, the British had been attacking American ships, and Clay was vocally in support of war, generating significant support for the War of 1812. Militarily, it proved to be largely a stalemate, which was a successful outcome for America and Clay. By holding off the British a second time, it became clear to Europe: America truly was a stand-alone nation. The Revolution would not be reversed. Inside the United States, the war generated a renewed sense of patriotism that had faded as the founding grew distant. This national spirit created momentum for Clay to start implementing his American System.

Working with Calhoun, Clay passed the only protective tariff to have significant backing from Southern states who, given their agrarian economies, did not see the need to protect US manufacturing. Clay also passed the charter for the Second Bank of the United States. Clay was implementing his economic agenda. However, America's major moral failing, slavery, continued to haunt the nation and Clay's work.

As our founding fathers built the Constitution, the question of slavery was at the forefront. The Southern economy was dependent on slavery, and they would never join the union absent its existence. However, many Northerners abhorred slavery. Even though many founders believed it evil, they decided uniting America was the foremost concern and accepted slavery in the South with the "three-fifths compromise" where only three-fifths of the slave population would count towards representation. It was wrong, of course, to count a slave as less than a human, but the North feared the South having too much power in Congress if slaves were counted fully.

In some ways, Clay was the right man to strike compromises between the slavery and abolitionist camps, for he shared the same moral confliction as our founders. On the one hand, he was from a slave state and owned slaves himself. On the other, he favored gradual emancipation and eventual end to slavery, even granting his own slaves their freedom when he died. Clay faced the first slavery crisis in 1819. At the time, the nation was divided evenly with eleven free and eleven slave states. Missouri sought to be admitted as a state, which would tilt the balance of power to the slave states.

Over the next year, Clay brokered an agreement. Maine would be accepted as a free state, keeping it balanced, twelve to twelve. Moreover, Missouri would be the last state above the 36.3 longitude mark allowed to have slaves. This meant that as the nation continued its westward march, northern states could be continued to be admitted to offset any new slave state. The battle lines between the North and South were forming, but Clay held the Union together.

In 1831, having already served as Secretary of State for John Quincy Adams, Clay returned to Congress, this time as a senator, to preserve his American System as the leader of the National Republicans against President Andrew Jackson. He would lose the 1832 presidential election to Jackson in a landslide, and the Second Bank would eventually be closed. Additionally, ever-higher tariffs were increasingly unpopular in the South. In 1833, South Carolina decided it would "nullify" the tariffs, essentially arguing it could overrule federal law, prompting President Jackson to ask for the power to send federal troops in.

Fearing Civil War, Clay acted as the critical go-between to a president he reviled and South Carolina's Calhoun. He forged a compromise—the Tariff of 1833—that would gradually reduce the tariff but also give the president the power to use force if a state ignored federal law. This compromise preserved the union, averted civil war, and reaffirmed the supremacy of the federal government. Clay put aside his personal differences with the president, secured a deal, and saved the union—or at least delayed civil war.

Feeling he had done his work, Clay retired in 1842, but he returned to the Senate in 1849 as he saw the nation dangerously divided over slavery once again. And so, he crafted one final agreement, the Compromise of 1850. Clay struck a deal where California, despite stretching to the South, would be a free state, and the federal government would assume debt from Texas, a slave state. It tightened fugitive slave laws, so Southerners did not have to fear slaves fleeing to the North, but also barred bringing slaves into America's capital, Washington DC, to be sold, an important symbolic gesture. This combination won support from all factions, even if each disliked specific provisions, holding the Union together a bit longer.

Clay had a vision of an enlarged America, with one national economy and domestic industrial might. He shepherded the nation through perilous moments, averting civil war or the Union's dissolution on several occasions while creating a more cohesive economy. By his death in 1852, America stretched from coast to coast with thirty-one states. He negotiated with all parties, on behalf of presidents he supported and opposed. If Clay had lived longer, one can only wonder if he would have helped to avert the Civil War. For his role in ensuring America would endure beyond its founders, Clay earned the title of the "Great Compromiser."

Ruth Bader Ginsburg

Supreme Court Justice

March 15, 1933 — September 18, 2020

On August 10, 1993, at the age of sixty years old, Ruth Bader Ginsburg was sworn into the United States Supreme Court, making her the second woman after Sandra Day O'Connor to serve on America's highest court. Ginsburg, a reliable member of the Court's liberal wing, would become a significant figure among the modern Left, often for her strong dissents in close decisions on the generally conservative Rehnquist and Roberts Courts. No one reaches the Supreme Court without being an intellectually gifted and very driven individual. This is particularly the case for Ginsburg, and her drive can be a source of inspiration for Americans of all political persuasions.

Born in Brooklyn in 1933, Ginsburg was raised in a time when most American women were expected to be housewives, not primary breadwinners. In 1951 when Ginsburg turned eighteen, men were nearly three times more likely to work than women with just one in three women participating in the labor force. However, Ginsburg's mother, Celia Bader, believed her daughter should be whatever she wanted. Celia had been an excellent student, but she lacked the resources to go to college; she did not want the same for her daughter. She believed deeply in the empowerment that a good education provides and encouraged her to study, took her to the library, and provided every resource she could.

Suffering from cancer, Celia passed away the day before Ginsburg graduated high school. While she did not live to see her daughter graduate, she had much to be proud of with Ginsburg enrolling at Cornell University. While at Cornell, Ruth met her future husband, Martin Ginsburg, and they married a month after her graduation.

She followed her husband to Harvard Law School where she juggled parenting a one-year-old daughter with her studies, even in the face of sexist behavior from school administrators. She was one of just nine women in a class of five hundred. She quickly made an impression and worked on the prestigious Law Review. When her husband got a job in New York City, she transferred to Columbia where she would graduate first in her class, all while being a mom.

Graduating first in the class from an Ivy League school would make one think Ginsburg could have any job she wanted, but in 1960, there were still many sexist attitudes about a woman's place. Thanks in part to strident help from a professor, she secured a clerkship for a district judge in New York. In her spare time, she even managed to learn Swedish so that she could publish a book on Swedish legal procedures, which she completed in about two years. In 1963, Rutgers hired her as a professor. At this time, there were no more than twenty-five female law professors in the country, and the school paid her less than a male professor even though she did the same work. Their explanation to her was that she should earn less because her husband also had a good job as a lawyer, giving her a personal experience of discrimination in the workplace. In 1972, now an established thinker in the legal profession, Columbia hired her as a professor.

During her career and her life, Ginsburg saw first-hand discrimination on the basis of sex, situations where women were treated differently because they were women. Her mother couldn't go to college. She faced sexist professors, struggled to get her first job despite being valedictorian, and, when she worked at Rutgers, made less than her male counterparts. So, while working at Columbia as a professor, she also began working for the American Civil Liberties Union (ACLU) on sex discrimination issues.

In her life, Ginsburg had fought against prejudice one item at a time, outworking the competition and scored incremental wins. That strategy takes patience, endurance, and determination, but it can prove very successful. She took the same strategy at the ACLU. Rather than seeking a sweeping ruling in the courts, which she could lose and which would set her cause back years, she focused on narrow laws that had explicit discrimination. She would argue six cases in front of the Supreme Court and win five. She even, at times, argued cases where men were being discriminated against, to increase her likelihood of winning while setting a precedent that sex-based discrimination was unconstitutional.

For instance, the Social Security Act only permitted special payments to widows with children—not widowers—a case where men were treated worse than women. In a unanimous opinion, the Court ruled this illegal. In a 1971 case, *Reed v. Reed* about the administration of estates, Ginsburg's brief to the court convinced the justices to rule that the Fourteenth Amendment, which promises "equal protection of the laws," bans discrimination based on sex. With these rulings throughout the 1970s, Ginsburg played a pivotal role in ensuring women received equal protection under the law at a time when more and more women were going to college and entering the workforce.

In 1980, President Jimmy Carter nominated Ginsburg to the DC Appeals Court where she would work with conservative judge Antonin Scalia. Scalia would ascend to the Supreme Court in 1986 where Ginsburg would rejoin him seven years later following a nomination by President Bill Clinton. Scalia and Ginsburg often had diametrically opposed legal interpretations with fiery dissents, particularly later in their careers. Despite their differing opinions on constitutional matters, the two would grow quite friendly, even spending each New Year's Eve together, bonding over shared interests like the opera. Their friend-ship can serve as a reminder that individuals with vastly different political views can share a fundamental love of country and enjoy each other's company.

On the Supreme Court, Ginsburg would continue to take the lead on sex discrimination issues—for instance, authoring an opinion that struck down a male-only policy at the Virginia Military Institute. She also has ruled in favor of abortion rights, gay marriage, and restrictions over the government's search and seizure powers.

Contemporary views of Ginsburg's judicial rulings are largely colored by one's political views, and history will have more to say on that legacy. Clearly though, her drive to overcome unfairness in her own life and to elimi-nate it from American society can inspire even those who disagree with her rulings as a Supreme Court Justice. For, there is little that is more truly American than working hard and working on behalf of others. Thanks to her drive to create a fairer world and her ability to overcome the inequities she faced in her life, American women that followed Ginsburg do not face the same inequities that she did and enjoy far stronger legal protections, making America a better and fairer nation.

Lyndon B. Johnson

President

August 27, 1908 — January 22, 1973

*I*n 1960, at the Democratic National Convention in Los Angeles, Massachusetts Senator John F. Kennedy, riding a wave of public support, secured the party's nomination for that year's presidential election. Kennedy offered the vice president slot to the runner-up, Lyndon B. Johnson. Johnson was Senate Majority Leader at the time, having served in Congress since 1937, giving the young Kennedy an experienced running-mate to balance out the ticket. Additionally, Johnson hailed from Texas, and his presence on the ticket would help them compete in Southern states.

Johnson delivered his home state of Texas and much of the South in a closely fought general election campaign against then Vice President Richard Nixon. The Kennedy-Johnson ticket would win the popular vote by a mere 0.17 percent, though the margin in the electoral college was a more decisive 303-219. Having served his primary purpose of getting Kennedy elected, the relationship between the two men was fraught from 1961 to 1963.

Technically, the Vice President has very little actual power and is only as influential as the President allows him to be, so in some ways, the job felt like a demotion for Johnson from being the Senate Majority Leader as he had been. In addition, Johnson and Robert Kennedy, the President's brother and attorney general, had a particular dislike for each other. Still, Johnson was given oversight of the NASA mission to land a man on the moon, and he became a forceful advocate for more aggressive action on civil rights issues, which was ironic as his presence on the ticket served to win support from conservative Southern Democrats who were more wary of that movement.

Everything changed on November 22, 1963, when President Kennedy was assassinated in Dallas, Texas, immediately ascending Johnson to the Presidency. For the preceding twenty-five years, Johnson had steadily accumulated power in Washington, and now, in a time of national mourning, he was the President.

Seizing the moment in an address to Congress shortly after Kennedy's death, Johnson declared, "No memorial oration or eulogy could more eloquently honor President Kennedy's memory than the earliest possible passage of the Civil Rights Bill for which he fought so long." With the relentless drive that had fueled his political rise, Johnson focused himself entirely to the cause of civil rights. In the summer of 1963, Kennedy had sent a civil rights bill to Congress, but it had gone nowhere. This bill would make discrimination based on race, sex, and religion a federal crime.

Members of the House and Senate have numerous ways that they can keep bills from coming up to the floor for a vote, from withholding unanimous consent, filibustering, filing rules objections, or holding it up in committee. These processes can help to safeguard bills from being rushed through without deliberate and adequate debate, but they can also be used to obstruct activity. Johnson was intimately familiar with parliamentary procedure, having been a skilled tactician in both the House and Senate. In fact, as Senate Majority leader he had mastered many of the techniques that opponents of the bill were using.

Consequently, Johnson maintained a multi-front strategy to force Congress to vote on his civil rights bill. First buoyed by increased national unity after Kennedy's passing, Johnson used the bully pulpit afforded a President to boost support for the bill. He worked with civil rights leaders like Dr. Martin Luther King to lobby for the bill, and he actively reached out to white religious leaders to win their support.

While building public support for the bill, Johnson used arcane congressional tactics against the obstructionists. By getting behind a "discharge petition," those members in favor of the Civil Rights Act could take control of the House of Representatives to force a vote on the bill. This caused the House Rules Committee to let the bill onto the floor, and it passed 290-110.

Johnson had also cleared the path for passage in the Senate. By backing a tax reform bill used by civil rights opponents to consume floor time, Johnson let the tax bill pass to open the floor for debate. He then maneuvered to keep the civil rights bill out of committee. Working across the aisle with Republicans, Johnson mustered enough votes to overcome a filibuster led by Southern Democrats, passing the first major civil rights bills in decades by a decisive margin of 71-29.

In 1965, after winning a massive electoral victory over Arizona Senator Barry Goldwater, Johnson dedicated himself further to the cause of civil rights and racial equality by pushing the Voting Rights Act. The Selma Marches and violent response by the police had further galvanized the nation against bigotry and the remnants of Jim Crow laws, sparking Johnson to address Congress to demand the passage of voter protections. After a ten-week fight, Congress passed the bill, which enfranchised millions of black voters by providing national protections for voters. From 1965 to 1967, in jurisdictions that faced additional federal oversight due to the bill, the percentage of black Americans who registered to vote rose from 29 percent to 52 percent, making it among the most effective pieces of civil rights legislation in history.

Using every tactical trick he knew, capitalizing upon his bully pulpit, and aggressively lobbying individual members of Congress, Johnson had muscled two of the most transformative pieces of civil rights legislation in history, making America a fairer nation and achieving the goals of a civil rights movement that had begun a decade before. While his drive to win at all costs won him a transformative victory on civil rights, it would also end Johnson's political career. In 1968, Johnson was eligible to run for reelection, but the war in Vietnam weighed considerably on his popularity.

The war, begun in earnest with a US ground operation in 1965, had become intractable and costly, causing inflation to move steadily higher after 1967. Johnson had become so invested in the conflict that he personally was choosing bombing targets out of the Oval Office, micromanaging the conflict like a piece of legislation through Congress. But, he could not control military outcomes like parliamentary battles. As a consequence, he stepped aside from the reelection fight, and his Vice President, Hubert Humphrey, would lose a close election campaign against Richard Nixon.

After his presidency, Johnson retired to his Texas ranch where years of smoking weighed on his health, and he died of a heart attack in 1973. But thanks to his relentless drive to fulfill President Kennedy's platform on civil rights, America became a far fairer nation, a legacy that extends to this day.

George H.W. Bush

President

June 12, 1924 — November 30, 2018

George H.W. Bush served as America's forty-first President from 1989 to 1993, though his service to this country began far earlier in his life. Quite possibly, no man has walked into the Oval Office as president with more experience in public life than Bush, giving him a unique set of experiences and personal relationships to guide America through some of the most consequential years in world history.

Bush was born into a wealthy New England family in 1924. Determined to protect his nation, immediately upon graduating high school and turning eighteen, Bush enlisted in the US Navy where he would become a pilot. He nearly didn't see a day of combat, having to crash-land a fighter jet while training in Virginia. His plane was destroyed. Fortunately for America, Bush was unscathed.

Five days shy of nineteen, Bush received his wings, becoming, at the time, the youngest fighter pilot in Navy history. Between enemy fire and technical problems, serving in the air was among the most dangerous assignments of World War II. About one quarter of America's dead—one hundred thousand men—in the second World War were airmen.

Bush was undeterred by the danger. Starting in May 1944, Bush began serving combat missions in the Pacific. During his time, he would fly fifty-eight missions and spend over twelve hundred hours in the air. One mission in particular is of note. Upon reaching his target of Chichi-Jima, Bush's plane was hit by enemy anti-aircraft fire. He still successfully dropped bombs on the target and bailed out into the ocean, concussing his head and tearing his parachute in the process. Stung by countless jelly-fish, head-aching, and stomach upset from drinking saltwater, Bush clung onto a life raft for hours until a US submarine finally rescued him.

Many men would not have had the will to survive, but Bush was not prepared for his life to end in the Pacific Ocean. Bush would later say that these events made him ask himself, "Why had I been spared and what did God have in store for me?" Bush had more to give his country, and this gift of life gave him the drive to serve America in the aim of building a more peaceful world.

After the war ended, Bush would marry the love of his life, Barbara, and develop a successful career in the oil business. From 1967 to 1971, he was a member of the

House of Representatives. A failed 1970 Senate campaign in Texas seemed to put the brakes on his career in elected life. But in 1971, Richard Nixon made him America's Ambassador to the United Nations.

When Gerald Ford became president after Nixon's resignation, he turned to Bush to become the special liaison to China with whom the US had only recently developed relations in an effort to check Soviet influence and power. Between the China assignment and his UN post, Bush began to develop contacts with global leaders.

Given his strong public reputation, Ford appointed Bush Director of the CIA to restore public faith in the institution after the intelligence failures and mistruths of Vietnam. Finally, from 1981 to 1989, Bush would serve as Ronald Reagan's Vice President, watching and learning as Reagan worked relentlessly to give America the upper hand over the Soviet Union and bring an end to the Cold War.

Holding onto a life raft, throwing up for hours, that young George Bush never could have imagined that forty-five years later, he would be sworn in as President of the United States, having just won an electoral land-slide, 426 to 111. Having seen and suffered the horrors of war firsthand, Bush had spent the previous twenty years in critical foreign policy roles, making friends and allies with diplomats, intelligence officials, and heads of state. Bush would need to use his deep foreign policy Rolodex over the next four years.

The Cold War between the Soviet Union and the United States was the defining geopolitical struggle ever since 1945 with two incompatible worldviews: free-market democracy and communist oppression vying for global supremacy. At times, it seemed like the struggle would go on forever, and there were moments, like the Cuban Missile Crisis, where nuclear war seemed inevitable. By 1989, thanks to a stronger economy, America had the upper hand. Still, no one could predict what was about to happen.

The Soviet Union had asserted near-total control over Eastern Europe up through 1989, but suddenly, by the end of the year, the system was in collapse. Most notably, on November 9, the East German government no longer enforced border checkpoints. The Berlin Wall, the starkest example of the Iron Curtain, was being torn down. Within a year, Germany was unified. Poland, Hungary, Czechoslovakia, and numerous other countries were set free.

Thanks in part to Bush's deft diplomacy, most of these political revolutions occurred peacefully, without a shot fired. These revolutions set in motion the collapse of the Soviet Union into the Russian Federation by 1991. The Cold War was over, and the US never had to fire a shot.

At the same time, trouble was brewing in the Middle East. Iraq's Saddam Hussein invaded Kuwait to expand its oil reserves. The disaster of Vietnam, a decade-long war that came at great cost with no victory, still haunted the American memory; there was great aversion to being entangled in another quagmire overseas.

Bush was intent on enforcing international laws, but his years of diplomatic work made him understand the importance of coalition building. Following the invasion of Kuwait in August 1990, Bush orchestrated global economic sanctions on Iraq, hoping for a peaceful resolution. In November, Bush gave Iraq until January 15, 1991 to exit Kuwait. During this time, he worked the phones and drew on his long friendships to build a coalition that would expel Iraq from Kuwait by force. Thirty-four nations contributed troops, Japan and Germany provided financial support, and even the Soviet Union gave public backing to Bush's coalition. In months, Bush had built the largest coalition since World War II.

Bush launched an aerial and naval campaign on January 17. Ground troops were deployed on February 24, and it took only four days to liberate Kuwait, one of the most stunning and lopsided military victories in history. Notably, Bush did not advance into Iraq; the mission was simply to restore national boundaries, not to topple existing governments.

As a young man, Bush helped America win a war. As a president, he oversaw a victorious war, one whose quick and decisive victory was critical in wiping out the malaise that still lingered in America's psyche from Vietnam. Bush spent his life driven to justify his survival from that plane crash over the Pacific. His years in public life during the 1970s and 1980s made him the right man to lead America during the political tumult emanating from communism's collapse and Iraq's aggression. In 1945, Bush wondered why God had spared him. Today, we know why.

Chapter 7:

Industriousness

Andrew Carnegie

Businessman

November 25, 1835 — August 11, 1919

*I*n the late 1800s, America would enter its second industrial revolution. During this revolution, America would complete its transformation from a largely agricultural economy to one built upon manufacturing. It was during this period that America would catapult forward among the world's nations as a leading industrial power. This economic revolutionary period has also been called the Gilded Age. While industrialization led to extraordinary growth with real wages rising by 60 percent from 1860 to 1890, it also saw a tremendous buildup in wealth and inequality. At this point in American history, the federal income tax had yet to come into effect, further widening the wealth gap.

Underpinning this industrial revolution was the growth of the railroad. Buildouts of the railroad network across the nation made it much cheaper to move people and goods, increasing demand for products. Before the railroad, it could take months to ship goods from New York to California; with the railroad, it could be done within days. More products increased the demand for more railways. And of course, what do railroads need but steel to lay down the tracks and make the railcars. The Gilded Era was *steel's* golden era. And if one was buying steel in the late 1800s, Andrew Carnegie was probably the man selling it.

Carnegie was born in Scotland in 1835 to a working-class family. Like so many immigrants, his family had fallen on hard times and made the long sail across the Atlantic to the United States of America in search of a better life when he was twelve. Upon coming to America, they settled down in Allegheny, Pennsylvania.

To help make ends meet, Carnegie worked in the cotton mill for twelve hours a day—not uncommon in those times even though he was barely a teenager. He continued to work any job he could find, and by 1849 had doubled his pay by working for the telegraph company, but he was still earning less than one hundred dollars per week in 2020 terms. By bringing telegraph messages, Carnegie was able to develop relationships with businessmen across the region, earning their respect. One man, a Colonel Anderson, even let Carnegie read from his personal library on weekends to better himself.

In 1853, seeing the impending boom, Carnegie began to work for the railroad. Within six years, at just twenty-four years old, he was overseeing the Western Division of the Pennsylvania Railroad. He had safely entered the middle class, earning nearly $45,000 per year in 2020 terms. Most critically, he saved every dollar he could and used the connections he had made as a messenger boy to invest in fast-growing companies that he would otherwise not have had access to.

In 1864, Carnegie shifted his focus away from the railroads to iron, realizing that the rails and coming industrialization would consume unprecedented amounts of it. He used his connections with the Pennsylvania Railroad to secure contracts building bridges for them. Over the next two decades, he continued to expand, investing the vast majority of his profits back into his company. He developed a new converter, which allowed him to much more rapidly and consistently convert pig iron into steel, and quickly undercut competitors on price, becoming the primary supplier to the railroad. He then used profits to vertically integrate his company, owning coking coal and iron mines and the steel mills to process it.

By owning all the layers of production, Carnegie enjoyed economies of scale. In other words, his company's large, integrated size meant he could produce steel more cheaply and his business had less exposure to volatility in commodity prices. In 1883, he acquired one of his main competitors, Homestead Steel, giving him another plant and a fleet of riverboats to transport his steel across the country. By 1892, he had renamed his company Carnegie Steel, and thanks to his massive investment in the industry, America was producing more steel than the United Kingdom. His steel industry provided the fuel for the rapid growth of factories and even provided the steel for America's new navy.

In 1901, Carnegie was sixty-six years old; he had worked just about every day in his life, starting with nothing and building the largest steel company in the world due to his hard work and relentless networking. Wanting to retire, he sold his company to J.P. Morgan, who put together several steel businesses to form US Steel, which still produces steel to this day. Carnegie was paid over $225 million, which, relative to the nation's economy at that time, would be equivalent to about $375 billion today.

Carnegie is a premiere example of the success one can achieve in America with hard work and a little bit of luck. His extreme wealth, aided by the lack of taxes, also was an example of the extreme inequality that arose during the Gilded Age as industries were born and companies quickly consolidated into behemoths and eventually monopolies. However, Carnegie never forgot his humble beginnings, and wanted to ensure that young and future Americans would have the same opportunity that he enjoyed.

In 1889, Carnegie wrote an article entitled, "The Gospel of Wealth" in the *North American Review*. Carnegie was acutely aware of angst around increased inequality; with the rise of populist figures like William Jennings Bryan, inequality was becoming an issue of extreme social contention. Carnegie argued that the wealthy should use their excess wealth to aid society rather than pass it down entirely and create an aristocracy. He felt that wealth should not be used to create a life of "slothfulness" and instead that the rich should be industrious in putting their talents back into society.

Carnegie capped his own salary at $50,000 (still greater than $1.5 million today), but of course, his equity ownership of his steel company generated significant wealth, if not annual income. When he sold Carnegie Steel, he became a fulltime philanthropist. Over the course of his retirement, he would give away over $350 million, virtually every penny he had ever made. As a young boy, Carnegie had been fortunate to have access to Colonel Anderson's personal library. Knowing the power of reading and access to education, he built over three thousand libraries across the world, democratizing access to education.

He also founded the Carnegie Institute of Technology (now Carnegie Mellon), served on the boards of Stevens Institute of Technology and Cornell University, and funded Booker T. Washington's Tuskegee University to educate black Americans. A lover of the arts, he built Carnegie Hall in Manhattan, and he created pension funds for his employees and American teachers, which exists to this day as TIAA-CREF.

Andrew Carnegie stands as a living embodiment of the American dream. Born with nothing, he rose to the pinnacle of industry, earning tremendous wealth, and then he worked just as industriously to use that wealth to help others. Originally born in Scotland, he led a truly American life.

Milton Hershey

Businessman

September 13, 1857 — October 13, 1945

*I*n 1929, as the stock market collapsed and a decade of financial exuberance came undone, America entered the Great Depression, the most painful and long-lasting economic collapse we have ever suffered. Over nine thousand banks failed, wiping out upwards of $200 billion of savings. Millions lost their homes and became reliant on government welfare programs that President Franklin Roosevelt began to implement in 1933. The unemployment rate rose to 25 percent, and America's economy would not really get back on its feet until the mobilization for World War II caused an unprecedented surge in industrial production.

Facing hardship, most businesses pulled back as demand for their products waned, resulting in layoffs, which cut demand further, forcing further layoffs. This vicious cycle helped turn recession into depression. Business stopped investment in capital expenditures, trying to preserve cash rather than grow their business. One businessman did the opposite. In fact, he saw opportunity to expand more cheaply, given the cost of most goods had fallen due to the depressed level of economic activity. His name was Milton Hershey.

Hershey was born in Pennsylvania in 1857, just before the outbreak of the Civil War. His parents operated a family farm, as was common in those days, and he worked the farm from a young age, learning the importance of hard work. His father would often travel, so Milton dropped out of school in the fourth grade to work the family farm and support his mother. Having been fired from his job at a newspaper, he secured an apprenticeship from a local candy maker at the age of fourteen. Over the next few years, he would travel to Philadelphia, New Orleans, Denver, and elsewhere to learn all about the candy-making business.

Borrowing capital from the local bank, he opened the Lancaster Caramel Company in 1883. Within a few years, the company was a tremendous success, allowing him to pay off all of his debt. In 1900, he sold the company for $1 million as his travel to Chicago had piqued his interest in chocolate.

At the time, milk chocolate was an expensive delicacy, and Hershey wanted to make it for the masses, so he purchased farmland in Lancaster, Pennsylvania, to secure a steady supply of milk. Later that year, he produced the first Hershey's bar, and in 1907, he was manufacturing Hershey's Kisses. His chocolate factory was surrounded by milk farms, and he became the primary driver of the local economy, building out the local infrastructure with schools, roads, and houses.

By 1918, Hershey had become one of America's leading businessmen. He had gotten married in 1898 to Catherine Sweeney, but they were unable to have children and she passed away in 1915. With no children to pass down the business to, Hershey decided to use his fortune to help society and transferred control of the company to a charitable trust. As a consequence, most of the Hershey Company's profits would go to charity, even though it was a for-profit company, primarily aiding education institutions like the Hershey Industrial School.

When the Great Depression struck, Hershey saw the economic devastation spread across the country as businesses and consumers pulled back. Hershey's business took a hit as well, but it was not as severe as most industrial companies, given the relatively low cost of his product. By this time, the area around his factory became known as Hershey, Pennsylvania, an unincorporated town.

Hershey viewed it very much as his own town, and he did not want to see it suffer like so many others were. No one was building houses, for instance, so construction workers were losing their jobs. Hershey realized that with no one building, the costs of building materials, from cement to lumber, were plummeting. If one had money, which he did, there was never a better time to start construction because one could complete projects at a fraction of the cost from a year earlier. And so that is what Hershey did.

He launched the "Great Building Campaign" to improve the quality of life for residents and create tourist attractions. He built a hotel, theatre, arena, golf course, new amusement park rides, and stadium. Hershey had wanted to do these projects in the past, and now was the perfect time. Moreover, because there were so many looking for work and costs were so low, he made sure these projects maximized employment. Famously, when he was told a steam shovel did the work of forty men, he ordered they stop using the steam shovel and hire more men. As a consequence, the residents of Hershey, Pennsylvania, did not suffer like the rest of the country. Hershey was one of the few companies in America not to lay anyone off. Because Hershey believed in the importance of work, he made sure everyone had jobs and turned his town into one of Pennsylvania's top tourist attractions, growing its long-term economic potential.

In many ways, the national response to the Great Depression came to mirror Hershey's own. As part of his New Deal, Roosevelt launched massive infrastructure projects to employ Americans and improve the country, doing everything from building the Hoover Dam to electrifying the Tennessee Valley. Indeed, many economists now recommend infrastructure spending as one of the most effective ways governments can counteract economic downturns, and such plans have been used frequently in America's history.

Hershey was no economist, but he well understood the importance of hard work. He had gone from working a family farm as a child to becoming one of America's wealthiest men, working hard to build one of the most beloved companies in the nation. He combined his good business sense with his philanthropic spirit to push against the forces of the Depression, keep his employees on the job, and improve life in his town. Hershey understood the importance of work and employment, and his successful experiment is now a model of how to help workers in a downturn.

Hershey died in October 1945, having led an extraordinary life and was one of the few men alive to see both the end of the Civil War and America's victory in World War II. To this day, the Hershey Trust Company, the charitable foundation Hershey had started, controls the Hershey Company with over $13 billion to support charitable work. Hershey's life is a testament to the value of hard work and the philanthropic potential it can generate.

Bing Crosby

Singer, Radio Actor, Film Actor

May 3, 1903 — October 14, 1977

*I*t takes extraordinarily hard work, loads of talent, and a little bit of luck to reach the pinnacle of any profession, let alone multiple professions. But Bing Crosby was no ordinary man. From the 1930s to 1950s, Crosby would be, at different times, America's leading singer, radio star, and movie star, starring in everything from silly comedies to critically acclaimed dramas. Crosby so dominated America's entertainment landscape, it would be like combining the stardom of Howard Stern, Taylor Swift, and Tom Hanks into one person. Fittingly, he has three stars on the Hollywood Walk of Fame for his success in radio, film, and music. Remarkably, in 1948, his career's pinnacle, half of all songs played on the radio were Bing Crosby songs.

Much of Crosby's success can be attributed to an unmatched work ethic, amassing a catalog of over one thousand six hundred songs with one hundred six albums. From 1940 to 1956, thirteen of his films finished in the top ten at the box office, making him one of the more reliable box office draws for Hollywood. He also did at least one weekly radio show from 1931 through 1958. Bing Crosby was America's biggest media star because he was the hardest working man in show business.

The fourth of seven children, Crosby was born in Tacoma, Washington, in 1903. Working at the local auditorium as a teenager, he began to develop a true love of show business, and he dropped out of Gonzaga University after three years to pursue his dreams. In 1925, he and his partner Miles Rinker moved to Los Angeles to pursue a singing career. With Crosby's smooth baritone voice, they quickly found work, and while performing in front of young crowds, he began to develop a charismatic and affable stage presence. By 1926, they were signed by Paul Whiteman, a major star at the time, and were making $150 a week.

Joining with a pianist, Harry Bailey, Crosby's group became known as "The Rhythm Boys" and scored a number one hit in 1928, *Ol' Man River*. However, over the next two years, Crosby became the clear star of the group, doing more and more solo numbers, and in 1931, he launched his solo career. Ten of the top fifty songs in America that year were his, beginning a steady stream of solo success. In 1932, he starred in his first film, *The Big*

Broadcast, the first of fifty-five times he would get top billing in a film. He would begin to steadily make three films a year on top of his radio show and music recording.

During the Great Depression, his strong sales single-handedly helped keep the record industry afloat. He also dramatically altered the economics of the industry, accepting a royalty on each sale rather than a flat fee. This made him more successful when he had big hits but would cost him if he had a flop. This payment structure became the norm for all artists, cutting the price of a record by over half, which further helped to support sales during the economic malaise. From 1931 to 1945, Crosby sold over sixty million albums according to conservative estimates.

In 1941, he scored perhaps his biggest hit with "White Christmas," which became a staple of the Christmas Season ever since. He capitalized further on that song by performing it in a 1942 film, *Holiday Inn*, boosting sales yet again. By appearing across all different forms of media, he created a self-perpetuating cycle of success.

His nightly and weekly radio shows became the primary way he interacted with the American public. Two decades before mass adoption of the television, radio was the primary form of nightly entertainment in most households. He produced his radio shows as elaborately as film directors constructed their set with a mix of songs and comedic routines. His Thursday shows were so popular that whatever songs he chose to perform were certain to be staples at nightclubs the following weekend.

In the 1940s, having established himself as America's top musical star, his film career took off, starring in a series of "Road To" comedy films with Bob Hope that showcased the comedic talents he had developed as a young performer on stage. Cheap to produce, they were consistently profitable box office draws. A talented actor, he won an Oscar for 1944's *Going My Way* while the 1945 sequel, *The Bells of St. Mary's* became one of the highest grossing films of all time.

In addition to being a star, he was a pioneer and entrepreneur, investing in one of the first tape recording companies. Up through 1945, nearly all radio shows were done live, and that meant Crosby had to do two shows per night—one for the East Coast and one for the West Coast. If he could pre-tape a show, he would only have to do one per day, and he could record a second time if there were mistakes or edit down sketches to improve the quality of his show. After a brief fight, he switched over to recorded shows in 1945, and his popularity only grew. Soon, recording shows would become the norm. He also used income from his royalties to diversify into owning local TV stations. A lifelong sports fan, he owned a piece of the Pittsburgh Pirates, bred racehorses, and hosted the PGA Tour tournament at Pebble Beach.

Between 1931 and 1954, Crosby had charting singles every single year, three hundred ninety-six songs in total. At his peak in 1939, he had twenty-four charting songs and by 1960, passed two hundred million records sold. In fifteen different years, he was also one of the top ten grossing actors. During the 1900s, only John Wayne and Clark Gable sold more movie tickets than Crosby. There were many days that Crosby was on a film set, recording songs, and doing a radio show, and because of that unparalleled work ethic, he enjoyed successes like no other entertainer in American history.

A proud patriot, Crosby also spent much of World War II touring across the European front to perform before Allied soldiers; a poll of soldiers ranked him first, above even President Franklin Roosevelt, in terms of lifting their morale. Crosby also taped broadcasts on behalf of the American Army that were projected into Germany to sway morale there.

After the 1960s, Crosby's career slowed down considerably as he enjoyed retirement. When he passed away in 1977, he achieved success that no other American entertainer would eclipse. There would be great music, radio, and movie stars, but none who would dominate each medium and do so for a decade. Only Elvis Presley would come close. Proving that hard work pays off, Crosby truly was the great entertainer of the twentieth century.

Thomas Edison

Businessman and Inventor

February 11, 1847 — October 18, 1931

*I*n the second half of the 1800s, America would be the center of the world's innovations, enjoying extraordinary growth after the Civil War up through the turn of the century. In an era of great inventors and innovation, Thomas Edison stands foremost among them for the magnitude and duration of his impact. During his life, he held nearly eleven hundred patents covering everything from the lightbulb, for which he is most famous, to electric engines. He would start at least fourteen businesses, chief among them, General Electric, which would spend decades as America's largest industrial company.

Edison was born in 1847 in Ohio, the youngest of seven children. He had essentially no formal education, spending less than one year in school. His mother had been a teacher, and she taught him reading and writing at home. Edison was a curious child who read voraciously on his own and was constantly experimenting and tinkering with inventions at home. Due to a case of scarlet fever, Edison became practically deaf when he was just a teenager, which he later came to view as a blessing as it allowed him to work without distraction more easily.

He began working from a young age, selling food and newspapers on the trains to Detroit, and he used most of the fifty dollars a week he was making to buy equipment for his experiments. He also worked as a telegraph operator and sold newspapers. At nineteen, he moved to Kentucky, working as a telegraph operator for Western Union, an easy job that gave him plenty of time to work on his experiments. By 1869, Edison had virtually no money to his name, but he had just registered his first patent, a machine to record votes electronically.

For the next few years, Edison worked on telegraphs, the preeminent means of communication at the time; his years as an operator had awakened him to the fact they could only send or receive one message at a time. He invented one that could send two at the same time, greatly boosting productivity. Western Union, his former employer, paid him $10,000 (over $200,000 today) for it, which is twice what he hoped to sell it for. With the profits, he opened a research facility in Menlo Park, New Jersey, where he would employ other scientists to help advance his inventions. Today, research parks are a common feature at innovative companies and institutions, but in 1876, his was the first of its kind.

Over the next decade, the Menlo Park facility would go on to employ dozens of America's top scientists and expand to cover two city blocks, developing inventions for utilities, chemical companies, and consumers. Edison would spend days at a time in his laboratory, working on his next big idea, and he drove his employees to work just as hard, making him a challenging boss. However, his drive led to extraordinary results that transformed society.

In 1877, Edison invented the phonograph, a machine that could record and replay sound. At first it had minimal use as the sound quality was not particularly good, but there was no invention like it, which marveled the world and spurred inventors like Alexander Graham Bell and others to adapt it and sell to consumers. Similarly, Edison invented the first motion picture camera, laying the groundwork for a movie industry that would begin to develop in the early 1900s.

However, Edison's grandest invention without a doubt was the lightbulb. It is hard to overstate how important the lightbulb was to industrialization and modern life. Lightbulbs enabled factories to be larger and run overnight, it transformed leisure time at home at night, and made it easier for nightlife options like restaurants to expand. Up until this point, society was dependent on candlelight and later, in cities, gaslights to function after dark. The sheer volume of candles also meant that fires were much more prevalent than they are today.

Given how life-altering and how large a commercial market there would be for an electric lightbulb, there was a multinational race among inventors and corporate titans to develop the first incandescent lightbulb. Edison had begun his experiments in his Menlo Park facility in 1878. Edison focused on expanding the life of bulbs as consumers couldn't afford to change out bulbs every day. By using a filament made of bamboo, he could make a lightbulb last over twelve hundred hours, and he filed a patent on November 4, 1879.

Partnering with J.P. Morgan and other financiers, Edison launched the Edison Electric Light Company, which would later be renamed General Electric, to produce his bulbs. He then needed to develop companies that could distribute electricity across cities and towns to provide power to the lightbulbs. And so were born the first electric utility companies, namely Edison Illuminating (a precursor to today's Consolidated Edison in New York). Over the next decade, Edison would build out electric power plants and electric utility networks to supply power for lightbulbs.

In 1892, Edison Electric merged with Thomson-Houston, and the company was renamed General Electric. At that time, the company had dozens of power stations, giving it control over three-quarters of the US electricity market. Just given the sheer size of this country, electrification was a massive undertaking that powered economic growth and productivity gains for decades. Dense cities received electricity first as the economics were much more favorable. It would take about forty years, until 1920, for the majority of American households to get electricity, and it would not be until New Deal projects in the 1930s for the number to near 100 percent.

While the incandescent light bulb was his greatest invention, Edison remained active the rest of his life, getting involved in rubber production, rechargeable electrical batteries, and mining. Given his interest in inventing rather than financial matters and the capital intensity of electrification, his stakes in his companies became rather small, and while he was likely worth close to $500 million in today's terms, he did not amass the same fortunes as other leaders during the Gilded Age, even if his inventions were more consequential.

In 1931, Edison passed away, suffering complications from diabetes. There were few days in his life where he didn't work. From starting out selling food on trains to building electric utilities, he was an entrepreneur and tinkerer at his core. Working day and night, he won America the race for a long-lasting incandescent light-bulb, setting in motion industrialization and the dawn of modern life.

Lee Iacocca

Businessman

October 15, 1924 — July 2, 2019

*T*he Chrysler Company was founded in 1925 by Walter Chrysler. The company was at the forefront of engineering and technical progress, even creating a new rim for tires that would become the standard across the entire industry. By 1936, Chrysler had the second most US sales among all carmakers, a status it would hold until 1949. Throughout the 1960s, the company would expand, developing a larger operation in Europe and selling larger vehicles under the Dodge and Plymouth brands.

However, the 1970s were challenging for the company. Gasoline prices skyrocketed after Middle Eastern nations embargoed oil, causing lines at gas stations and shortages. As prices at the pump soared, consumers preferred smaller, more fuel-efficient cars. At the same time, government regulations were increasingly stringent to make cars safer and better for the environment. By now, Chrysler was the smallest of the Big Three US automakers, having been overtaken by its Detroit rivals, General Motors and Ford. Foreign car manufacturers were also making gains, selling one out of every five cars in the US by 1979. Poor quality of its vehicles also left Chrysler with significant warranty and repair costs.

So, in 1978, Chrysler turned to a Detroit veteran, Lee Iacocca, to turn its fortunes around. Iacocca was born in Eastern Pennsylvania to a family that operated a hot dog restaurant. He would go on to study engineering at Lehigh University and take a job at the Ford Motor Company in 1946 where he rose through the ranks due to his natural talent for marketing. He was critical in developing the iconic Ford Mustang and returned the company to greatness in the racing world with Ford cars winning many major races under his stewardship.

His relentless focus on strong operations and visionary marketing made Ford a financial powerhouse. While Chrysler bet on gas guzzlers, he expanded Ford's footprint in small cars, positioning it well for a period of high gas prices. He became the company's president in 1970 and led the company through the volatile period so well that they generated $2 billion in profits in 1978.

Amid increased tensions between Iacocca and the Ford family, he was fired in July 1978 despite the company's strong financial performance. Given his tremendous track record, the challenged Chrysler board immediately pounced and hired Iacocca as their Chief Executive Officer. While Chrysler was the smallest automaker, it was still a gigantic corporation, the tenth largest in America with three-hundred-sixty thousand employees at the company and throughout its dealership network. In addition to automobiles, the company was critical to American national security, manufacturing the Abrams tank, for example.

When Iacocca took over Chrysler, the company was in desperate shape. Years of mismanagement had left it with a bloated cost structure and poor quality control. Its smaller size made it harder for the company to invest in research and development to improve fuel efficiency. Strategically, the company's product lineup was simply poorly positioned for consumer tastes. As a consequence, the company faced a $500 million loss that year.

Iacocca knew that Chrysler was too important to fail. Countless middle-class Americans relied on the company, directly or indirectly, for their livelihood. By improving management and sharply shifting strategies, he believed the company's best days could be ahead of it. But given its massive losses and the investment needed, he knew it would be costly—money the company didn't have. Worse, the company's pension was $800 million underfunded, jeopardizing the retirement security of thousands.

So, in 1979, Iacocca turned to the US government to ask for a federal bailout. There was strong pushback to risking taxpayer money to help a private company. It was not the government's job to protect companies from their own mistakes after all. However, the economy was already struggling with high inflation, and a recession loomed. A Chrysler bankruptcy, wiping out tens of thousands of jobs, would only worsen the economic crisis, particularly in the industrial Midwest.

Iacocca presented Congress with a three-year turn-around plan, and they approved a guarantee of $1.5 billion in loans. With this federal guarantee, banks were willing to lend to Chrysler again, giving it much-needed cash to invest in its operations. Alongside $1.5 billion of federal support, its private investors and employees chipped in $2 billion to reduce its expenses and debt.

With financial breathing room, Iacocca set about the work of saving Chrysler. In 1981, the company launched its "K-car," small cars that were inexpensive and fuel efficient. Iacocca had hoped to make them at Ford but had been blocked by the family. Given the recession the country faced, these more affordable cars sold extremely well. Iacocca also launched the minivan in 1983, which became the top-selling vehicle in America.

Iacocca gave Chrysler a product that customers wanted while investing to ensure quality was once again up to standard. These changes caused a rapid turnaround in its finances. In 1980, its market share had fallen to 9.3 percent, selling barely one million vehicles. By 1984, its market share was up to 11.3 percent, and it passed 1.6 million vehicles sold.

Thanks to help from the government and his drive to make the company succeed, Iacocca turned around Chrysler, saved over one-hundred thousand jobs, preserved an iconic brand, and gave consumers more choices when buying an automobile. In 1983, Chrysler paid back its guaranteed loans seven years ahead of schedule, absolving taxpayers of financial risks. Rather, the federal government made over $250 million in profits from its involvement in the Chrysler bailout.

By 1984, Chrysler was solidly profitable, earning $2.4 billion in profits. Iacocca would remain CEO until 1992, by which time the company had expanded further, acquiring Jeep, and continuing to increase its market share, to 13.3 percent.

In 1979, many were prepared to write off Chrysler as a once-great American company whose best days were behind it due to foreign competition, inept management, and new regulation. Instead, Iacocca believed in the company's future, laid out a vision, and got the government, investors, and the union to buy into it. What followed was an extraordinary turnaround and rebirth of an industrial giant, which provided good jobs and livelihoods to thousands.

The story of Chrysler under Lee Iacocca is a stark reminder that working hard to achieve a strategic vision can lead to tremendous success. America's history is littered with examples of underdogs who prevail; indeed, our victory in the Revolutionary War ranks among the greatest underdog stories in history. The story of the 1979 Chrysler bailout is just another reminder to never count out the industriousness and ingenuity of the American worker when given the resources and vision to succeed.

Chapter 8:

Innovativeness

James Madison

President

March 16, 1751 — June 28, 1836

*T*oday, democracy seems like an obvious concept. Of course people should have a say over who their government is. The government should work for the public, and if they do an unsatisfactory job, they should be voted out. Most great ideas seem obvious after they've been implemented, but they often start out as new and controversial. When we think of innovation, we usually think of science or technology. But the very idea of the American government—that the government gets its rights from We the People—was a remarkable innovation.

Up until 1776, monarchy and aristocracy were the norm. America endeavored to be something entirely different. Nearly two-hundred-fifty years later, the genius of this innovation is self-evident, not only by America's own success but by the fact that most of the world has moved toward democracy. Perhaps more than any other founding father, James Madison deserves credit for the successful implementation of this innovation.

Born in 1751, Madison was only twenty-five years old when the Declaration of Independence was signed. The Articles of Confederation were ratified by the thirteen colonies in 1781, but they left the federal government exceptionally weak. America was less one nation of states than an association among states. As a member of Virginia's House of Delegates, Madison felt the Articles needed to be reformed to strengthen the national bonds.

As the 1780s progressed, it became increasingly clear to all that Madison's concerns were correct. So, in 1787, a convention was held in Philadelphia to draft a new constitution. Madison crafted the Constitution, and then, working with John Jay and Alexander Hamilton, he wrote essays, which we now call The Federalist Papers, to sway public opinion in favor of the new constitution.

Madison, though, faced a problem. History was filled with examples of men who promised to give power to the people but instead took more for themselves. Power corrupts. Here, Madison developed the greatest innovation in American government, which he outlined in Federalist 51: an intricate system of checks and balances. He believed the government needed to "control itself."

How exactly do you do this? Madison realized he needed to give different aspects of government different powers. They would then guard those powers against each other. Congress, the legislative branch, would have the power to pass laws and spend money. The president, the executive branch, would implement and enforce the laws as well as oversee the military. The courts, or the judicial branch, would rule on legal disputes, ultimately through the Supreme Court.

Importantly, each branch had the ability to counter the others. The president could veto laws Congress passed, but Congress can impeach and remove the president from office if he is deemed to have committed a "high crime or misdemeanor." As we will discuss next when learning about John Marshall, the courts can rule a law unconstitutional, but members of the court are nominated by the president and confirmed by the Senate.

So, each branch had distinct powers and the ability to push back against each other. Equally important, Madison ensured they had incentive to work together. The president needs Congress to allocate money for him to implement his agenda. Congress relies on the president to enforce the laws they pass, and while the courts can issue rulings, they need the president to act upon their rulings.

Beyond the checks and balances of the federal government, the Constitution also leaves powers to state government, primarily to regulate commerce within their state borders and "police powers." This is why most crimes are state offenses, not federal ones. And if a state feels the federal government is treading onto their powers, they can sue for the courts to determine who is in the wrong. Thus, there are checks and balances within government and between governments.

This innovative structure was built to ensure that a power-hungry leader could not reverse the American experiment. No one branch of government, let alone one person, could trample on Americans' rights and reverse our democratic principles.

Going even further, to win the support of those still worried the government had too much power, Madison drafted the Bill of Rights, the first ten amendments to the Constitution. These amendments enshrined the right to free speech, religion, and a fair trial, among others. Unlike other nations, Madison did not craft our laws so that governments would bestow rights on their citizens— rights that could someday be taken away. Instead, these amendments made clear that these were *God-given rights*, upon which the government could not infringe. And if the government made a law that did so, citizens would have the clear legal right to have it removed. These amendments provided the last check against government power.

It was only fitting that Madison's Virginia would be the tenth state to ratify the constitution, giving it the necessary 75 percent support to become America's foundational law. At just thirty-seven years old, he shepherded a constitution that would serve America to this day. Now, America is the oldest representative democracy on the planet. Through our challenges and ups and downs, the innovative structure that Madison built ensured that we have not slipped into dictatorship. Instead, our success has inspired more countries to follow our lead and adopt democratic processes of their own.

While Madison's greatest, most innovative legacy was the crafting of the US Constitution with its checks and balances, he had more to do. He served as a member of the House of Representatives and became secretary of state. He would go on to serve as America's fourth president from 1809 to 1817, successfully navigating the nation through the War of 1812 with England. After his presidency, he retired to private life, though he occasionally weighed in on public issues. Most notably, he forcefully argued against the concept of nullification—that a state could secede from the union. To his dying day in 1836, Madison believed we were one United States of America.

America is an innovative nation because the very idea of America is innovative. The idea that government works for the people and that the people grant their government rights, not the other way around, was revolutionary. Madison did more than any other founder to make this dream an enduring reality by developing a finely-tuned government structure so that no entity could gain too much power at another's expense. This innovative system of checks and balances has come to define American government and ensure the survival of democracy.

John Marshall

Supreme Court Justice

September 24, 1755 — July 6, 1835

*T*ypically, when we think of innovativeness, we think of the first to do or be something, but that's not always the case. In John Marshall's, it wasn't. Little known today outside of legal circles, Marshall is among the most influential men in American history, whose innovative view of the Supreme Court has shaped the nature of American democracy. In fact, no study of James Madison's checks and balances is complete without a study of how John Marshall solidified them as America's fourth chief justice of the United States Supreme Court.

Marshall was born in a rural portion of colonial Virginia in 1755 and spent his childhood in a two-room log cabin, the oldest of fifteen siblings. Like another American luminary raised in a log cabin, Abraham

Lincoln, Marshall received no formal education. In 1775, he volunteered for the Virginia Regiment and joined the Continental Army in 1776.

Completing service in 1780, Marshall began studying law and was admitted to the Virginia state bar, becoming a recognized attorney. He began his political career in 1782, winning a seat in the Virginia House of Delegates. In the 1780s, he worked with Madison to build support for a new constitution that would put the power in the hands of the people while cementing the primacy of the federal government over the states in many matters. Following the adoption of the new constitution, Marshall focused on his private law practice.

In 1800, President John Adams nominated Marshall secretary of state, after which, Marshall helped to end an undeclared naval war with France that began two years earlier after a controversial diplomatic visit to France—one which Marshall himself had been involved in. This naval war had destroyed America's shipping industry. It was this conflict that had bankrupted Elizabeth Ann Seton's husband.

At the end of 1800, Chief Justice Oliver Ellsworth resigned given his failing health. Adams wanted to nominate John Jay, the nation's first chief justice, but he refused because he did not believe the Supreme Court was powerful enough. So, Adams turned to Marshall. Marshall would soon show how short-sighted Jay was.

Marshall became chief justice on February 4, 1801, a post he would hold for thirty-five years. If Madison was an innovator when it came to constructing a government with checks and balances, Marshall was the great innovator when it came to ensuring its survival. Madison had created three branches of government, but at times, it felt like the judicial branch was a junior partner compared to the legislative and executive. The president controlled the army and enforced laws while Congress controlled the spending and could write laws. When Marshall took over, the Supreme Court merely occupied a single room in the US Capitol building.

Marshall, though, saw a way to ensure the judiciary would be a co-equal branch, and ironically, James Madison would be involved. President John Adams had lost reelection to Thomas Jefferson, and in the final days of his presidency in 1801, he filled several open judgeships, which the Senate quickly confirmed. However, a few of the judge commissions were not delivered by the time Jefferson was inaugurated. Jefferson ordered his secretary of state, Madison, not to deliver the remaining commissions. William Marbury was one of the nominees, and he sued to get his commission delivered so that he could serve.

The details of the case seemed quite minor, but Marshall had the case he was looking for. Today, you will often hear that the Supreme Court either rules a law constitutional or strikes it down as unconstitutional. However, the power to do so is never explicitly laid out anywhere in the Constitution. Instead, John Marshall invented it.

Marshall saw one problem with Madison's checks and balances. What would happen if Congress passed a law that violated the US Constitution? The president could potentially veto it, but perhaps he agreed with the law, or Congress could override the veto. Was the Constitution just a set of governing principles that Congress could ignore, or was it actual law?

Marshall determined that not only was the Constitution law; it was the supreme law of the United States, meaning that if any law contradicted the Constitution, the Constitution wins, and that law is null and void. Because it is the court's job to interpret the law, and the Constitution is a law, it is the court's job to determine if laws are constitutional or not.

In *Marbury v. Madison*, Marshall found a portion of the 1789 Judiciary Act contradicted the powers the Constitution gave the Supreme Court. And so, in the first example of "judicial review," Marshall struck down that part of the law.

In the end, the Supreme Court did not give Marbury the ruling he wanted, but the specific facts of the case are not why this case is among the most important in our nation's history. Rather, it served as the vehicle by which Marshall determined that the Supreme Court could invalidate congressional laws as unconstitutional with a portion of the Judiciary Act being the first casualty of judicial review. By providing an effective check against congressional overreach, Marshall ensured the judiciary would sit as a co-equal branch of government alongside the executive and legislative. This legal innovation was critical to ensuring the implementation of Madison's checks and balances.

Over the next thirty-two years, Marshall would continue to lead the Supreme Court until his death in 1835. During this time, his rulings would cement the *Marbury v. Madison* precedent, that the Constitution is the supreme law of the United States, prevailing over any contradiction with federal law, and that federal law was supreme over state law, helping to solidify the legal union of states.

We often don't realize it, but more mundane innovations are often necessary to make the first one work. Yes, the automobile was a tremendous innovation, but it never would have grown popular without the invention of the gas station and pumps to quickly fill tanks. The idea of gas pumps was essential for automobiles to gain mass adoption.

Similarly, Marshall's judicial review innovation was critical to make the judiciary a co-equal branch of government and ensure there was sufficient check on Congress's lawmaking power. Of course, Supreme Court rulings are not infallible, and at times, it has been necessary to overturn past decisions. However, Marshall's innovation has ensured that the Constitution is the supreme law of the United States. By doing so, he helped guarantee that America is governed by laws and not by the whims of politicians.

Orville and Wilbur Wright

Inventors

August 19, 1871 — January 30, 1948
and
April 16, 1867 — May 30, 1912

Orville and Wilbur Wright were born in 1871 and 1867, respectively, to a middle-class family. The family moved around constantly as their father was a bishop, though they eventually settled in Dayton, Ohio. As children, they loved to tinker, particularly with a toy helicopter, which, once broken, they learned how to fix. Neither of the brothers would graduate high school.

Serial inventors, Orville had built his own printing press, and the two started a weekly newspaper in 1889, and then in the mid-1890s, they opened a bicycle repair shop. They later even produced their own bicycles. The profits they made selling bikes would go on to fund their own experiments with flight. Flight had been a dream of man for centuries, with Leonardo da Vinci even trying to devise of a machine that could fly during the Renaissance. By the 1890s, technology was beginning to catch up with these ambitions. Germany, with pioneering efforts by Otto Lilienthal, had become a leader in gliders before his death during an accident testing a model, and there were numerous efforts in the American government and private sectors to achieve flight.

Because they were not scientists, the Wright brothers took an incrementalistic approach to flight. While the leading theorists of the day were developing large engines without ever having flown personally and trying to attach them to a winged frame, Orville and Wilbur started building gliders and testing them themselves to see how they operated empirically. They studied how birds leaned their bodies during turns and developed wing-warping, a series of cables that allowed the ends of the wings to twist.

In 1900, the brothers began a series of trips to Kitty Hawk, North Carolina, to test their models and planes. The area was sufficiently windy, and because the terrain was sandy, models that crashed would not be badly damaged, making it cheaper and quicker to repair them. Because they were funding their experiments with income from their bike business, it was crucial to be economical.

By 1902, after two years of testing, the brothers had discovered much more about how much lift was needed to get a plane airborne. After testing over two hundred wing designs, they discovered that they needed wings that were longer and narrower to generate less drag on the plane while also making the wings flatter than past models. When they tested out these findings at Kitty Hawk, it was a success. They were able to control the glider in the air for the first time in October 1902. Having now discovered how to make planes fly and control them in the air, they had perfected gliding. Now, it was time to build an engine for a powered plane.

Over the course of 1903, the brothers began building the Wright Flyer, using spruce wood given its relatively high strength to weight ratio. They built their own gasoline-powered engine in the bike shop and tested various propellers in their homemade wind tunnel, determining that two propellers would work better than one. They used aluminum to build the engine as the goal was to keep it as lightweight as possible. Rather than use a fuel pump, which would weigh it down, gasoline was kept above the engine so that gravity would feed it. Having developed these innovations over the course of 1903, they would be ready to test powered-flight later that year.

Meanwhile as the Wright Brothers were using their personal savings to build an airplane on a shoestring budget, the American government was also trying to achieve flight. Samuel Langley, who was Secretary of the Smithsonian Institution, was developing his own winged aircraft, which he dubbed an "aerodrome." By 1894, he had built small models that were unmanned and powered by steam, which managed to fly for nearly two minutes. Remarkably, these small tests caught the eye of Teddy Roosevelt, who was at the time Assistant Secretary of the Navy.

By 1898, the US military had contracted with Langley to build an aerodrome, starting with a $50,000 grant, which would be about $20 million today. This grant was in addition to the taxpayer funds that the Smithsonian already received, making it one of the costliest government research and development projects at the time. By 1901, Langley had a model built to quarter size that worked, and he built a full-size aerodrome in 1903.

To take off, the plane needed to be catapulted to gain sufficient speed. In an act of arrogance, Langley decided to have the plane fly off a ship on the Potomac River. On October 7, after it was launched, the plane fell immediately into the river, causing severe damage. It took two months to repair the aerodrome at taxpayer expense, and on December 8, they tried again, once more on the Potomac River. Yet again, it fell straight into the river because the frame could not handle the stress of the launch. It is easier to make costly mistakes when spending someone else's money.

The Wright Brothers returned to Kitty Hawk in late fall 1903 where they encountered several minor problems during tests of the engine. Wilbur tried the first flight on December 14, but the engine stalled after takeoff. However, because of the sandy terrain, there was only minor damage, allowing them to continue progressing forward. Finally on December 17, 1903, just one week after the second government failure, the Wright Brothers successfully completed four test flights, two each. In total, the brothers spent just about $1,000 to achieve what no one had ever done: manned, controlled flight. Two American bike mechanics had done what the leading governments and scientists could not.

The American economy has unleashed unrivaled innovation, often spurred by everyday citizens who have an idea and pursue it relentlessly. Our democratic values, which inspire people to think for themselves and take agency for their own actions rather than rely on direction from government, are inextricably linked to our innovative spirit and successes.

Orville and Wilbur Wright's success inspired countless Americans to pursue flight and aerospace. It is no surprise then, that the nation that was first to fly was the first to reach the moon. To this day, about 10 percent of America's manufacturing sector is related to aerospace. The Wright Brothers are a testament to the fact that anyone can change the world.

Henry Ford

Businessman

July 30, 1863 — April 7, 1947

An American did not invent the automobile. Karl Benz of Germany is widely credited with inventing the first car with an internal combustion engine in 1885. However, America invented the way to mass produce the automobile, and in the process, we changed the way products were manufactured. In the early 1900s, America became the world's greatest industrial power, building an industrial base that proved critical to the war effort in World War II. Much of this legacy is owed to Henry Ford.

Ford was born in Michigan during the Civil War in 1863. At the time, the horse and buggy was the dominant source of transportation, with the railroad just gaining scale. By Ford's death in 1947, the automobile would define America's transportation system, with most households owning at least one. A series of innovations Ford developed were critical to this transformation. From 1875 to 1925, the great economic shift in America was moving further from being an agrarian economy to an industrial one. It is only fitting that Ford himself was raised on a family farm, which he left to work as a machinist.

In 1892, Ford had built his first automobile and, after testing it for years, he built a second and third car at home by 1896. Confident in his models, in 1902, Ford partnered with Alexander Malcomson to begin building inexpensive cars, but sales were slow. Saddled with debt (after all, the costs to build even one car are expensive, given the necessary machinery, parts, and supplies), they brought in other investors, forming the Ford Motor Company. In 1908, the Model T was born. It cost a mere $825, about $25,000 today.

Dreaming of a car in every house, Ford wanted to drive down costs further and needed to increase productivity to meet demand. By this time, the concept of an assembly line had taken hold in American manufacturing. Rather than having to train one person to build a product from start to finish, it was better to have employees specialize in just one aspect of production. They would become better at that one task, and the product would be passed down a line for each worker to do their stage of production until it was complete.

In 1913, Ford innovated on this concept with the creation of a moving assembly line. Cars in production moved along conveyor belts, hastening their pace along the assembly line and regulating the speed at which employees worked. This transformed the efficiency of Ford plants, allowing him to churn out more cars at a lower cost than any of his competitors. While it originally took twelve hours to build a single car, his factories could now produce one in thirty minutes.

From 1914 to 1916, Ford nearly doubled production to 472,000 Model Ts. Equally impressive, a Model T in 1916 cost just $360, less than half of its price in 1908. In a world where prices generally rise, Ford's innovations in how cars were assembled were so powerful that he was making his product less expensive. Thanks to this innovation, he made cars available to the masses and not just the wealthy. As a consequence, he soon had 50 percent market share. One out of every two new cars on the road was a Model T.

Ford undertook several other initiatives to expand car ownership. While many auto manufacturers sold cars to the public directly, Ford built out a network of franchise dealerships. Building a dealership was costly and time-consuming, so he sold the right to sell Ford cars to other businessmen who would build a dealership, buy the Model T, and sell it to the public. This accelerated sales, and to this day, the use of franchised dealership networks is the predominant way Americans buy a car.

While Ford had a laser-like focus on reducing the cost of his cars, interestingly, he did not do so by undercutting his workers' pay. He believed that the average Ford worker should be able to at least afford the car that they were building. In 1914, as the moving assembly line was proving to work as effectively as hoped, Ford doubled the minimum wage his company paid to five dollars per day, about a $40,000 annual salary in today's dollars. By offering the best pay among automakers, Ford also enjoyed very low rates of staff turnover, which increased efficiency. He was also able to attract the best talent given how much more he was paying than competitors. Ford ensured that the profitable gains of his assembly line innovation would help not just his personal finances but those of his employees as well. In 1926, Ford moved to a five-day workweek (from six days previously), creating the norm that has endured to this day—that just about everyone, and not just the wealthy, should enjoy a two-day weekend.

Of course, this is not to suggest that Ford only sought to enrich employees and not himself. He used hardnosed negotiations to buy out all of the other owners of Ford Motor Company by 1921, and he used his better pay arrangement to hold off the unionization of his workforce until 1941, making Ford the last major automaker to unionize. Still, after the Gilded Age, which saw tremendous strides forward in American living standards alongside widening inequality, Ford practiced a new capitalism that sought to lift all boats, raising the living conditions of workers while also boosting corporate profitability.

The mass adoption of the car would not have been possible without Henry Ford's assembly line innovations, which made cars so much more affordable for middle- and working-class Americans. The mass adoption of the car also facilitated another social trend, the growth of the suburbs, which persisted over the next fifty years. Cars are needed to live in the suburbs given the commute to work, school, the grocery store, and so forth, after all. Absent Ford's efforts to make the automobile available to masses, the suburbs would not have become accessible for more as well. His moving assembly line was adopted not just by other automakers, but by manufacturers of radios, appliances, and other goods, greatly expanding Americans' ability to purchase them and creating the boom of the 1920s. From January 1919 to March 1927, America's industrial output rose by 40 percent, even though production to support the America's military in World War I ended.

Henry Ford is one of America's greatest innovators who helped propel America further into the industrial age as the world's leading manufacturing power. Additionally, he helped to dramatically raise the living standards of his workers with pay raises and a two-day weekend, innovations and concepts which have powered the American economy to this day.

Walt Disney

Businessman

December 5, 1901 — December 15, 1966

*W*ith a name that is now synonymous with quality family entertainment, no one has had as profound of an impact on the entertainment and media industry as Walt Disney. While the company has changed dramatically since his death in 1966, the Walt Disney Company is still the largest media conglomerate on the planet, with interests in everything from comic books to sports.

Disney was born in Chicago in 1901, though he spent much of his childhood in Missouri. In 1918, he wanted to help America in World War I but was too young. However, by changing his date of birth on his birth certificate, he was accepted as an ambulance driver. By the time he reached France, the war was over. Disney then returned to Kansas City, Missouri, after the war where he decided to make a living out of his passion, which was drawing. Disney drew commercial drawings for catalogs, advertisements, and so on.

From there, he began to study animation and moved out to Los Angeles to join his brother Roy and start his own business. After years of modest success, Disney had created a popular character, Oswald the Lucky Rabbit, but Universal Studios owned the rights to the character. When Disney refused a pay cut, most of his employees left him to work for Universal.

Shortly after this, Disney created Mickey Mouse in 1928, and the character became an instant success. The Mickey Mouse shorts, starting with Steamboat Willie, were not the first animated shorts, but they were the first with sound that was synchronized, a revelation in a movie landscape dominated by silent film. Those who had abandoned Disney would soon come to regret the decision, as Mickey Mouse quickly became one of America's most popular characters, and Disney would release a steady stream of successful animated shorts throughout the 1930s. He would also move to color animated shorts before the competitors. Disney consistently improved upon what was the market convention.

Then in 1934, Disney had a groundbreaking idea. Animated shorts had proven to be very popular, often shown in front of a film or as part of a collection of shorts. However, feature length films were exclusively live-action. Disney set out to make the first feature-length, hand-drawn animation film ever: *Snow White and the*

Seven Dwarfs. As it was the first film of its kind, Disney was intent on making it a smashing success, sparing no expense, even bringing animals into the studio so artists could study their movement to make the film looks as realistic as possible. Hollywood insiders thought Disney was making as career-ending decision that would result in financial ruin, calling it a "folly." The film ran well over budget, costing $1.5 million (about $30 million in today's terms) and took over two years to make.

Finally, in December 1937, Snow White premiered, stunning audiences and critics alike. The Oscars gave Disney an honorary Academy Award, and the film would not only be the most popular film in 1938, but briefly be the highest-grossing film ever, until *Gone with the Wind* surpassed it. Disney created an entirely new genre of filmmaking with animated films, beginning a career of smash-hit films targeted at children that their parents could enjoy as well.

Between his animated shorts starring Mickey Mouse and other characters and a string of popular films, the Disney brand become synonymous with quality, wholesome family entertainment. By 1950, he would branch into live-action films with *Treasure Island*. In 1952, unhappy with the small amusement parks he took his children to, Disney decided to build his own, beginning the process for Disneyland near Los Angeles. Rather than just a group of rides, he sought to build an immersive world, essentially bringing the wholesome environment of his films to life. Spending millions of his own money on the sprawling project, it opened in July 1955. A year after opening, the park had brought in over three million visitors.

In about thirty years, Disney had turned his one-room studio into a veritable media conglomerate with live-action and animated production for television and movies and now theme parks. Ever the builder, Disney always sought to do more. Throughout the late 1950s and early 1960s, the studio continued to churn out hits, most notably *Mary Poppins*, and Disneyland was becoming a bigger part of the company's profitability. However, the tight geography made it very difficult to grow the park very much.

To this point, amusement parks were largely local attractions. In fact, it was still quite popular for attractions, like the circus, to travel around the country to come to their audience. Disney wanted to invert this norm, building an all-inclusive world that people from around the country would travel to. By 1960, air travel was growing rapidly, and while still quite expensive, it was likely to continue to grow and become less expensive over time.

Disney needed to find a desolate location with cheap real estate and a climate suitable for year-round activity. He set his eyes on Orlando, Florida. However, if his plans became known, real estate costs would likely become much more expensive, so Disney secretly, and through a series of middlemen, began buying up as much property as possible. Finally, after having bought thousands of acres, in late 1965, rumors leaked out, and Disney confirmed them. He had a vision for multiple parks, hotels, golf courses, restaurants, and even a futuristic community modelled on his work for the World's Fair. And so, the idea of a family resort was born.

In December 1966, with plans well underway, Walt Disney passed away from lung cancer, and his brother, Roy, took over the project to ensure as much of "Walt's Dream" would come to fruition. The parks would open in October 1971, and to this day, Disneyworld is the most popular vacation attraction on the planet.

Disney innovated the very concept of family entertainment, making the first feature-length animated film. To this day, animated films are a bedrock of the movie industry with all major studios housing their own animation effort. Often, the greatest compliment to an innovation is the fact that others seek to replicate it. Disney followed this success by transforming the nature of amusement parks to make them more immersive and larger than ever before—a vacation destination in their own right. And with a collection of films and characters that endured in popularity for decades, he had an indelible impact on American and the world's culture, throughout the twentieth and into the twenty-first century. Walt Disney was a true American icon.

Conclusion

*T*here are clearly thousands of Americans whose lives would be strong examples of the eight American ideals we discussed in this book: resilience, daring, faith, fairness, sacrifice, drive, industriousness, and innovativeness. Hopefully, the lives of these forty Americans, with very different stories to tell, from authors to presidents to judges and prisoners of war, have helped you learn more about what it means to be an American and the story of our nation's history.

No nation is perfect, but what defines America is our constant striving to be more perfect, to live up to our ideals, and to be a land with more opportunity for more people than anywhere else on Earth. In their own way, each of these forty individuals helped to advance America and enrich our culture. Anyone who can learn from and model the great attributes of these men and women will lead a successful life.

Like our nation, these forty Americans are a diverse bunch, living in different times, white and black, male and female, conservative and liberal. At times, it might seem like there is more that makes them different than what makes them similar. But, that's only at the superficial level. Fundamentally, they have far more in common. Each man and woman on this list dared to dream that they could lead a life that matters and have an impact bigger than themselves—that they could change the world for the better. And that optimistic pursuit of a dream is what makes every one of them, at their core, an American.

In 1910, Teddy Roosevelt gave his famous "Man in the Arena" speech where he eloquently laid out his worldview:

> It is not the critic who counts; not the man who points out how the strong man stumbles, or where the doer of deeds could have done them better. The credit belongs to the man who is actually in the arena, whose face is marred by dust and sweat and blood; who strives valiantly; who errs, who comes short again and again, because there is no effort without error and shortcoming; but who does actually strive to do the deeds; who knows great enthusiasms,

the great devotions; who spends himself in a worthy cause; who at the best knows in the end the triumph of high achievement, and who at the worst, if he fails, at least fails while daring greatly, so that his place shall never be with those cold and timid souls who neither know victory nor defeat.

Simply put, it is better to do and fail than to live life on the sidelines, cynically criticizing the doers. Every one of the Americans in this book lived their lives in the arena, actively working to advance their ideals, making the nation better in the process. While we may not be able to control the success of our endeavors, we do control whether we step into the arena. To ensure we pass on a better America to the next generation, we must choose to do just that.

About the Author

Scott Ruesterholz lives in Florida where he works in financial services. His political commentary has been featured in numerous outlets like Townhall and The Federalist, and he has often been cited as a financial expert in numerous media outlets, including CNBC and the *Wall Street Journal*. He has previously written a novel, *Robert Wilson and the Invasion from Within*, which was published in 2021.